CAPE
YORK
PENINSULA

BARKLY TABLELAND

Leichhardt River

Flinders River

Todd River
• Alice Springs

SIMPSON DESERT

MUSGRAVE
RANGES

LAKE EYRE

Warburton River

Cooper Creek

STURT
DESERT

STURT'S
STONY
DESERT

Mackenzie River

GREAT DIVIDING RANGE

• Brisbane

LAKE TORRENS

LAKE
FROME

Darling River

LAKE
EVERARD

LAKE
GAIRDNER

FLINDERS
RANGE

Hunter River

BLUE
MOUNTAINS

GAWLER
RANGES

GREAT DIVIDING RANGE

Sydney •

EYRE
PENINSULA

Murrumbidgee River

Murray River

• Adelaide

Canberra •
MT. KOSCIUSKO •

SNOWY
MOUNTAINS

THE
GRAMPIANS

Melbourne •

WILSON'S
PROMONTORY

CRADLE
MOUNTAIN •

LAKE
GORDON

Hobart •

LAKE
PEDDER

AUSTRALIA

AUSTRALIA

By the Editors of Time-Life Books

TIME-LIFE BOOKS ○ ALEXANDRIA, VIRGINIA

Other Publications:

MYSTERIES OF THE UNKNOWN
TIME FRAME
FIX IT YOURSELF
FITNESS, HEALTH & NUTRITION
SUCCESSFUL PARENTING
HEALTHY HOME COOKING
UNDERSTANDING COMPUTERS
THE ENCHANTED WORLD
THE KODAK LIBRARY OF
   CREATIVE PHOTOGRAPHY
GREAT MEALS IN MINUTES
THE CIVIL WAR
PLANET EARTH
COLLECTOR'S LIBRARY OF THE CIVIL WAR
THE EPIC OF FLIGHT
THE GOOD COOK
WORLD WAR II
HOME REPAIR AND IMPROVEMENT
THE OLD WEST

This volume is one in a series of books describing countries of the world — their natural resources, peoples, histories, economies and governments.

For information on and a full description of any of the Time-Life Books series listed above, please write:
Reader Information
Time-Life Customer Service
P.O. Box C-32068
Richmond, Virginia 23261-2068

Cover: An aged desert oak stands alone in the flat landscape bordering a highway in the Northern Territory. In the background are the violet domes of the Olgas, ancient mountains worn smooth by erosion.

Time-Life Books Inc.
is a wholly owned subsidiary of

TIME INCORPORATED

FOUNDER: Henry R. Luce 1898-1967

Editor-in-Chief: Henry Anatole Grunwald
Chairman and Chief Executive Officer: J. Richard Munro
President and Chief Operating Officer: N. J. Nicholas Jr.
Chairman of the Executive Committee: Ralph P. Davidson
Corporate Editor: Ray Cave
Executive Vice President, Books: Kelso F. Sutton
Vice President, Books: George Artandi

TIME-LIFE BOOKS INC.

EUROPEAN EDITOR: Kit van Tulleken
Assistant European Editor: Gillian Moore
Design Director: Ed Skyner
Photography Director: Pamela Marke
Chief of Research: Vanessa Kramer
Chief Sub-editor: Ilse Gray

LIBRARY OF NATIONS

Editorial Staff for *Australia*
Editor: Tony Allan
Researcher: Krystyna Mayer
Designer: Lynne Brown
Sub-editor: Sally Rowland
Picture Department: Christine Hinze, Peggy Tout
Editorial Assistant: Molly Oates

EDITORIAL PRODUCTION

Chief: Jane Hawker
Traffic Coordinators: Alan Godwin, Maureen Kelly
Editorial Department: Theresa John, Debra Lelliott, Sylvia Osborne

Valuable help was given in the preparation of this volume by John Dunn (Melbourne).

Contributors: The chapter texts were written by Philip Beard, Windsor Chorlton, Alan Lothian and Craig McGregor.

Assistant Editors for the U.S. edition: Karin Kinney, Barbara Fairchild Quarmby

Pages 1 and 2: On page 1 is the emblem of Australia, consisting of a shield bearing the badges of the six states enclosed within an ermine border signifying federation. The crest is a seven-pointed star; six points represent the states and the seventh the nation's two federal territories. The shield is supported by a kangaroo and an emu, and the whole emblem is adorned with the wattle plant. The national flag appears on page 2.

CONSULTANTS

Professor Geoffrey C. Bolton, Head of the Australian Studies Center at the University of London, is the author of many books and articles about Australian history. He is the editor of the forthcoming five-volume *Oxford History of Australia.* Craig McGregor is one of Australia's leading social commentators and journalists. His books include *Profile of Australia* and *The Australian People.*

Second printing. Revised 1987. Printed in U.S.A.
Published simultaneously in Canada.
School and library distribution by Silver Burdett Company, Morristown, New Jersey.

TIME-LIFE is a trademark of Time Incorporated U.S.A.

Library of Congress Cataloguing in Publication Data
Australia.
   (Library of Nations)
   Bibliography: p.
   Includes index.
   1. Australia.   I. Time-Life Books.   II. Series:
Library of Nations (Alexandria, Va.)
DC96.A95 1986   994   86-5985
ISBN 0-8094-5165-4 (lib. bdg.)
ISBN 0-8094-5164-6

Front and back endpapers: A topographic map showing the major rivers, plains, mountain ranges and other natural features of Australia appears on the front endpaper; the back endpaper shows the country's states and territories, as well as the major cities and towns.

CONTENTS

In Sydney, Australia's oldest and largest city, the gleaming skyscrapers of the business district tower above wharfside buildings of an earlier era. In the

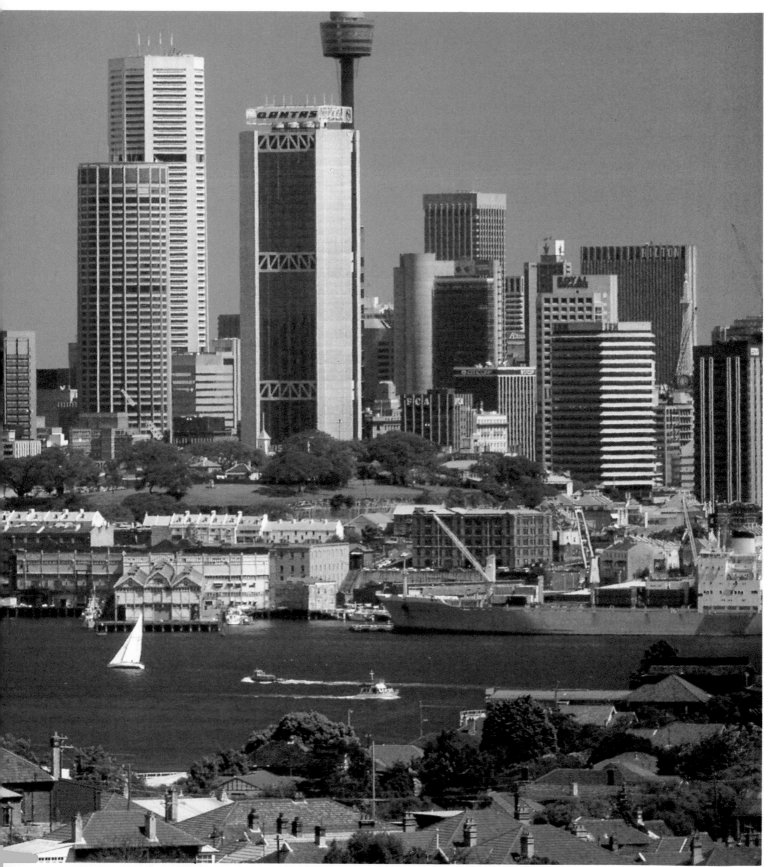

two centuries since British settlers first landed at nearby Sydney Cove, Australia has become a largely urban nation.

A LAND OF CLIMATIC EXTREMES

Over much of Australia, the climate is hot and dry. The continent lies at the world's most arid latitude, where subtropical high-pressure systems reliably produce day after day of clear skies. Rainfall is generally slight and the evaporation rate high. Surface water throughout the interior is scarce, and a huge band of desert sweeps across the center of the continent.

But great variations occur: The tropical north is influenced by the Northeast Asia Monsoon, and summer rains are heavy. The east coast is relatively well watered by the prevailing southeasterly trade winds, which shed much of their moisture over the Eastern Highlands. In winter, westerly winds bring high rainfall to the southwest and southeast coasts and to Tasmania.

TROPICAL

SUBTROPICAL

TEMPERATE

SEMIDESERT

DESERT

NORTHERN TERRITORY

QUEENSLAND

WESTERN AUSTRALIA

SOUTH AUSTRALIA

NEW SOUTH WALES

VICTORIA

TASMANIA

In a remote region of the Northern Territory, a tourist bus negotiates a dirt track through a rugged outback landscape. Since the 1970s, Australia's hinterland — little developed because of its low rainfall — has attracted a growing number of visitors, drawn by its austere beauty.

Refreshed by a morning swim, three Aboriginal youngsters relax near a Darwin beach. Thousands of Aboriginals perished under the initial impact of

A NATION OF CITY DWELLERS

Although they inhabit an entire continent, the 15 million people of Australia live close together. All but about two million are city dwellers. Even more unusual, approximately 65 percent are concentrated in eight cities — the six state capitals plus Canberra and Darwin, the main towns of the two federal territories. The chart above illustrates relative population density: Dark bars represent cities, lighter bars the surrounding state or territory.

colonization, but improvements in medical care since World War II have helped boost the population to about 200,000.

NEW-FOUND MINERAL WEALTH

Over the past two decades, Australia has emerged as one of the world's major mineral producers. In 1960, minerals accounted for only 7 percent of the country's exports; by the 1980s, however, the proportion had risen to around 40 percent. The nation had become the world's largest producer of iron ore, with reserves estimated at 20 billion tons.

The continent's energy resources are equally impressive: Economists coined the phrase "Lifeboat Australia" to convey the image of a secure, well-stocked refuge riding the stormy waters of international trade and diplomacy. Australia produces almost as much coal as Britain or West Germany and has unmined reserves estimated at 30 billion tons. Oil production is now running at some 400,000 barrels a day, which provides two thirds of the country's needs. Most of this comes from the offshore Bass Field between Victoria and Tasmania, whose yield is expected to decline sharply by the end of the decade. As a result, exploration is under way to find new fields.

Vast sums and much technical ingenuity are also being expended on tapping Australia's natural-gas reserves, which are thought to have greater long-term potential than the crude-oil reservoir. Each mainland state capital is already supplied with piped gas. Current plans are for only about 25 percent of production to be consumed domestically, leaving a large surplus for the export market.

A spectacular sunset casts its glow over fuel tanks on the waterfront at Fremantle, in Western Australia. Described by one 19th-century observer as the

resort of "rogues and drunkards," the port — now part of Perth's metropolitan area — has prospered as Australia's main gateway to the Indian Ocean.

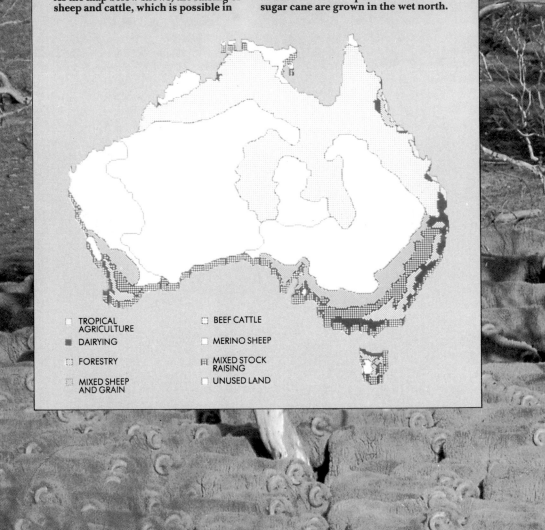

PATTERNS OF LAND USE

More than half of Australia is devoted to rural industries, but only 7 percent of the land is suitable for intensive use. As the map below shows, the raising of sheep and cattle, which is possible in relatively dry areas, is widespread; crop farming is largely confined to the moist coastal regions of the southeast and southwest. Tropical fruits and sugar cane are grown in the wet north.

TROPICAL AGRICULTURE

DAIRYING

FORESTRY

MIXED SHEEP AND GRAIN

BEEF CATTLE

MERINO SHEEP

MIXED STOCK RAISING

UNUSED LAND

A flock of hardy Merino sheep troop through a tract of outback scrub used, like 90 percent of Australia's agricultural land, in its natural state for

low-intensity grazing. Australia has about 15 percent of the world's sheep, and wool accounts for nearly one tenth of the country's export income.

1

Filling the approach road to the Sydney Harbor Bridge, rush-hour traffic crawls past the city's world-renowned Opera House. More than 85 percent of Australia's 15 million inhabitants live in cities and towns, with just over one car for every two people.

A COUNTRY COMES OF AGE

The first thing that strikes any newcomer to Australia is its size. To a visitor flying in from the north, the low, brown land stretching away almost featurelessly to the horizon can seem endless, and indeed the distances involved are great. With an area of 3,072,900 square miles and a coastline 22,041 miles long, the country is nearly as large as the United States, excluding Alaska and Hawaii. Sydney on the east coast is farther from Perth on the west than Barcelona is from Moscow.

The Australian continent is divided into six states, each with its own elected government with wide responsibility for local affairs. The largest state is Western Australia — four times bigger than Texas and 11 times the size of Great Britain — followed by Queensland, South Australia, New South Wales, Victoria and the island of Tasmania. The Australian Capital Territory, a small area surrounding the federal capital of Canberra, is directly ruled by the central government — as was the sparsely populated Northern Territory until 1978. Now the Northern Territory is a self-governing unit with powers similar to those exercised by the states.

In 1985, the total population of this vast land mass was a mere 15 million, or on average just five people for every square mile — less than one tenth the density of the United States and one hundredth that of crowded Great Britain. The reasons for this sparsity lie partly in history. For millennia the continent was inhabited exclusively by an Aboriginal population whose hunter-gatherer lifestyle did not encourage expansion; steady growth began only with the arrival of the first European settlers on the continent in 1788. But even more profound has been the influence of the land itself, whose unique features continue to shape the development of the nation to the present day.

Australia is the lowest and flattest of continents. More than 50 percent of the land is less than 1,000 feet above sea level; a mere 5 percent rises above 2,000 feet. It is the driest continent, if exception is made for uninhabited Antarctica. While the world's land surfaces receive an average of 29 inches of rainfall each year, Australia's annual precipitation is a niggardly 19 inches. This figure, however, is deceptive, because it conceals wide regional variations. A few areas, such as Tasmania in the south and parts of Queensland in the north, are well watered, with up to 160 inches of rain; conversely, huge parts of the interior and much of the west and central south may suffer drought for years on end, then receive flooding downpours.

The main explanation for Australia's aridity is its position, straddling the 30° line of latitude, where most of the world's deserts in both hemispheres are concentrated. Midway between the equatorial air mass to the north and the polar air mass to the south, Australia is subject to prevailing subtropical high-pressure systems — anticyclones — that bring successions of clear, sunny days and regularly raise temperatures in some parts to more than 90° F.

As a result, cloudy days and rainfall can be anticipated with certainty only on the fringes of the land mass. The far north receives summer rains from the edges of the Asian monsoon, while the southern extremities of Australia, on both the east and the west, benefit from winter rains as the sun retreats north of the equator, dragging the northern limit of the wet westerlies after it.

These winds, however, quickly lose their moisture as they move inland; indeed, in one area of Western Australia, the rainfall declines by almost an inch for each mile of territory covered. Only rarely does rain reach the center of the continent, where, to quote one small boy's answer to a question on an examination, "The climate in summer is such that its inhabitants have to live elsewhere."

With so much sunshine, the rain that does fall rapidly evaporates, leaving little water available for human purposes. Australia has one great river system, the Murray-Darling, which drains the western slopes of the southeastern highlands and provides water for large irrigation systems along its 1,600-mile length. Yet in a mere seven days, the River Ganges in India empties into the ocean more water than the Murray discharges in an entire year. The Amazon accomplishes the same task in one and a half days.

A hidden resource helps to alleviate the drought. One seventh of the water available for farming across the nation is buried deep underground in several artesian basins. One of these, the Great Artesian Basin, underlies more than one fifth of the continent north of the

Murray and Darling rivers, making it the largest subterranean reservoir in the world. Although artesian water is too saline for irrigating arable land, it is vital for watering livestock. About 20 percent of the nation's sheep — from the early days of European settlement a crucial part of the Australian economy — depend on artesian water supplies. More than 30,000 wells have been sunk to exploit this underground treasure; but since the rate of replenishment is slow and demand high, less than 10 percent of them are still in operation. Their outflow makes habitable areas of the continent that would otherwise remain desert, but it does not make them green.

The availability of water, more than any other factor, has determined the pattern of Australia's growth, with a populous coastal zone surrounding an interior that is eerily empty. A visitor from densely populated Western Europe or the congested cities of the Orient cannot fail to be awed by the scarcity of people in certain parts of the country, where neighbors may live several hundred miles apart and a trip to the nearest supermarket or movie or hospital can entail a round trip of 1,000 miles or more. This is the outback, whose brown and lonely expanses stretch over much of the Australian interior.

The outback's most distinguishing feature is the Western Plateau, a low tableland that emerges from Western Australia's coastal plains to cover almost all of that state, most of the Northern Territory, much of South Australia and a part of western Queensland. Some of the plateau is true desert, whether in the form of Sahara-like waves of rippled sand dunes or the more typical, boulder-strewn wildernesses Australians call gibber plains. Most of the Western Plateau is semidesert, a flat, parched tundra dotted with spiky clumps of spinifex grass and mulga and mallee scrub. Here the sun is an enemy and the wind can strike with the sudden heat of an opened oven door. In its less arid stretches, where rain or artesian bores permit other vegetation to grow, the tundra melds seamlessly into marginal pastureland. This is the territory of the great cattle stations, ranches that are the size of small kingdoms and that may cover three million acres.

Although the average elevation of the plateau is only about 1,000 feet, the monotony is relieved in widely separated locales by higher ground, notably in the Hamersley Range, whose tallest peak rises to 2,798 feet. Toward the plateau's northwestern rim are the irregular ranges of the Kimberley Plateau, a knot of hills about 1,600 feet high dissected by a maze of short river systems that make this one of the most rugged and inhospitable regions of Australia. Farther east are the gentler uplands of Arnhem Land, in the Northern Territory's "Top End," whose main river, the Katherine, drains westward through a deep, narrow gorge inhabited by fresh-water crocodiles. Toward the eastern rim of the Western Plateau are the Macdonnell, Musgrave and Petermann ranges, which are cut through in places by old riverbeds and often spectacularly weathered. Alice Springs, whose fame rests mainly on its position as one of the world's most isolated modern settlements, grew up around an artesian well in one such gap in the Macdonnells. From its origins as a station of the Overland Telegraph, built from Darwin to Adelaide in the late 19th century, Alice Springs has developed into a township of more than 50,000 people, with a casino and a tourist trade that uses it as a center for outback travel.

To the east, the Western Plateau comes to an end in a series of low drainage basins extending from the Gulf of Carpentaria in the north to western Victoria in the south. The average elevation of this belt, called the Central Eastern Lowlands, is less than 600 feet, but it falls to more than 30 feet below sea level at Lake Eyre. Heaven help the unwary traveler who expects to find water in this lake or in its tributary rivers, among them Cooper's Creek. Here, the explorers Burke and Wills perished of thirst and malnutrition in 1861 on their return south after making the first south-north crossing of the continent. By a savage irony, nature has

put Australia's biggest lake in the driest part of a dry continent. It has been known to fill only twice this century. Heavy rains in the early 1950s and early 1970s produced a body of water up to 40 miles wide and 80 miles long, with a brine that was saltier than the sea. Both times, however, the lake was soon reduced to a series of puddles surrounded by thousands of miles of salt flats. In 1964, British hydroplane-and-auto racer Donald Campbell set a world landspeed record on the lake's dry bed.

The Lowlands are rimmed to the east by the Great Dividing Range, which forms an intermittent girdle along the entire length of the continent's flank. With its frequent gaps and an average altitude of less than 3,000 feet, it is a barrier to communications only in the southeast, where Australia's highest mountain, 7,310-foot Mount Kosciusko, rises from the section of the range known as the Australian Alps — a major winter sports site containing the mainland's only snow-covered peaks. But the Eastern Highlands, as the range is known to geographers, do shelter the

most complex and varied landscapes in Australia. These include primeval tropical forests in northern Queensland, fantastic pinnacles formed by ancient lavas in the Glasshouse Mountains of southern Queensland, and the deep, ferny gorges and ravines of New South Wales's Blue Mountains — so called because of the bluish atmospheric haze produced by the exudation of oils from the ubiquitous eucalyptus tree.

Almost all of the water that seeps into the Great Artesian Basin and the Murray-Darling river system has its source in the Eastern Highlands. The range provides even more generously on its other, eastern flank, because easterly and southeasterly winds, depositing their moisture on its slopes, make the corridor between the mountains and the sea the best-watered and most fertile region of the continent.

Nowhere is this corridor more than 240 miles wide, and in places it shrinks to less than 30 miles. Yet it is on this narrow fringe, and its continuation along the margins of the south coast, that most of the population of the

THE MARSUPIAL MENAGERIE

A koala slumbers peacefully in the fork of a eucalyptus tree.

A baby gray kangaroo peers from its mother's pouch.

A hairy-nosed wombat leaves its burrow to feed in the coolest part of the day.

During Australia's eons of prehistoric isolation, animal life developed along different lines from the rest of the world. Marsupials — mammals that produce their young in virtually embryonic form and continue to nurture them in the mother's pouch — diversified to fill the evolutionary niches occupied elsewhere by placental mammals.

Today, the commonest marsupial is the kangaroo, of which there are 90 varieties, from the eight-foot-tall great red kangaroo to the tiny rat kangaroo, only 10 inches long. Kangaroos live on plants, as do most of Australia's other indigenous animals — the mild-mannered koala, for instance, lives exlusively on eucalyptus trees. An exception is the carnivorous Tasmanian devil, a doglike creature no longer found on the mainland.

The duck-billed platypus, an egg-laying aquatic mammal, is distinct from the marsupials. Also unique to Australia, it is — along with two types of spiny anteater — a survivor of an otherwise extinct order of mammals.

The quokka is the only kangaroo variety without a long, muscular tail.

A duck-billed platypus glides underwater.

The rare Tasmanian devil's unaggressive manner belies the animal's fierce name.

1

continent is concentrated — about 80 percent of the people occupying about 5 percent of the land. And it is here that the phenomenon of Australian urbanism — as evinced by the cities of Sydney, Melbourne and Brisbane, and such smaller centers as Newcastle and Wollongong — is best studied.

Climate and the availablity of water determined that all of Australia's state capitals — including South Australia's Adelaide, Western Australia's Perth and Hobart in Tasmania — would be built on the coast. The marine presence and the proximity of beaches have given them a unique and enviable ambience of relaxed hedonism. Many office workers structure their lives more or less around the thin yellow lines of sand that fringe the freeways, eagerly accepting an early starting time for the work day so they can get off at four o'clock in the afternoon to indulge in some serious sunbathing on the edge of the booming surf. One of the arche-typal images of today's Australia is of a clutch of teenagers, with sun-bleached hair, blue eyes and the complexions and figures that are the products of affluence, good nutrition and open-air living, clustered around an RV topped with upended surfboards or windsurfing equipment.

The easy outdoor mood extends to eating and socializing, where it usually takes the form of the great Australian institution, the barbecue. At lunchtime and at dinner, in parks, on beaches, and among the bougainvilleas and gladioli of a hundred thousand suburban gardens, the smell of charred steaks and chops and broiled sausages rises amid the hum of small talk and the clutter of thirstily emptied "tinnies," or beer cans. So popular is cooking out that concrete barbecue pits, equipped with two to four separate grills, are a common sight in public places. The habit of alfresco eating also extends to the stalls in the city streets that sell seafood: oysters, crabs, lobsters, mud crabs and small fresh-water crayfish called yabis. The beer required to wash down this picnic is kept cool by means of another relished convenience, the "eskie," or poly-styrene ice chest, which is automatically a part of the luggage for a majority of outdoor excursions.

The pattern of housing in the cities is, for the most part, extensive rather than concentrated, with a populace spread out around a central business area in often far-flung suburbs. Although apartment living is on the increase, the typical Australian home remains the detached house, with a strip of green at the front and a large yard in back. The suburbs have their own focal points in the form of shopping centers, typically built around three sides of a pedestrian area. On one side will be the supermarket, on another the post office; boutiques, or perhaps a municipal building or two, will fill the intervening spaces. Many shopping centers incorporate three-story malls, whose covered passageways serve less to keep off the rain, as is generally true in the Northern Hemisphere, than to act as glass-and-concrete sunscreens.

Among them, Australia's six state capitals house some 60 percent of the population of the country. The reasons they loom so large in the nation's life can be traced partly to the nuclear pattern of its growth and the rapid development of highly centralized administration, commerce and transport. Each of the six cities occupies the site where settlement began in its state. At the time, land in the interior was used primarily for grazing, rather than for intensive forms of agriculture, so there was little need for the development of large rural centers. Instead, the produce from each estate was funneled

GREAT NORTHERN HIGHWAY
EYRE HIGHWAY
STUART HIGHWAY
BRUCE HIGHWAY
BARRIER HIGHWAY
STURT HIGHWAY
OTHER MAJOR ROADS
MAJOR RAILWAYS

DARWIN
PERTH
ADELAIDE
MELBOURNE
HOBART
BRISBANE
SYDNEY
CANBERRA

The layout of Australia's major roads and railroads indicates the settlement pattern imposed by climate and geography. The arid interior supports only small, isolated towns, while the major cities enjoy the moister, cooler weather along the coast.

through its capital on the way to markets abroad. In consequence, all the people who were needed to service the trade, from merchants and shippers to bankers and insurance companies, established themselves there. When manufacturing started, the cities were chosen as its logical site; when road and rail networks were built, they inevitably led to and from the capitals. And as the six states became more independent of one another, economic rivalry sprang up between them, so that if one of the capitals expanded, the others tried to emulate it.

Personal inclination has also had a lot to do with the growth of the cities. A traditional Australian saying is "Sydney or the bush," with Sydney and its fellow cities representing affluence and a good time and the bush being equated with discomfort and poverty. In the early days of white settlement, the choice was a real one: to remain in Sydney and be surrounded by civilized amenities, ready work and social attractions, or to risk carving out a life in the inimical interior, where the promise of an independent lifestyle was counterbalanced by vagaries of drought and flood and a haunting loneliness. Most Australians chose Sydney, and the pattern of urbanization was set for the generations to come.

Sydney is not, of course, the capital of Australia; that honor belongs to Canberra, the city created as the seat of national government after the six states federated in the Commonwealth of Australia on January 1, 1901. But Sydney, with its 3.28 million people spread out over an area of 1,630 square miles, is the country's largest and most bustling metropolis. It can also reasonably claim to be the oldest, for it was at

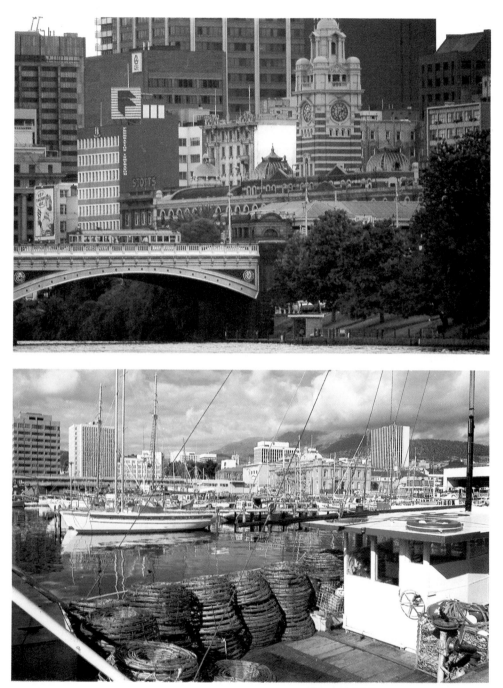

Although Melbourne *(top)*, the capital of Victoria, seems as tranquil as Hobart *(above)*, in Tasmania, Melbourne is a bustling, cosmopolitan city. Australia's six state capitals were founded within 50 years of one another, but each fiercely maintains its individuality.

Sydney Cove, one of the many inlets that indent its beautiful harbor, that Australia's first white settlers came ashore in 1788. The city still centers on the harbor, which the English writer Anthony Trollope described in 1873 as being "so inexpressibly lovely that it makes a man ask himself whether it would not be worth his while to move his household goods to the east coast of Australia, in order that he might look at it as long as he can."

Nature ensures that the city still retains its basic glamor, with 30 superb beaches along its eastern edge and an average of more than five hours of sunshine a day. Yet Sydney also suffers from many of the ailments of rapid and haphazard growth. The shores of Botany Bay, where Captain Cook's ship *Endeavour* dropped anchor in 1770, now shelter polluting heavy industry. Downtown Sydney — framed by those symbols of modern Australia, the Harbor Bridge and the Sydney Opera House — was extensively built up after World War II without sufficient planning for the increased traffic that development would bring. As a result, Sydney's one million automobiles thread their way between skyscraper canyons on roads that were never designed to take anything but pedestrians and horses. The cars have also helped to pollute the city; the sun cooks the hydrocarbons produced by internal-combustion engines and converts them to a photochemical smog that now rivals those of Los Angeles and Athens in its noxious intensity.

The most desirable residences in Sydney are the fine houses fronting the harbor, while the gentrified 19th-century enclaves of Paddington and Woollahra, with their cast-iron balconies and wooden shutters, have a peri-od charm that is especially popular with the affluent young. But the great majority of Sydneysiders, like the great majority of all Australian city dwellers, live in the middle and outer suburbs. Give or take a few details, the houses there follow a nationwide pattern, accurately and devastatingly described by writer Craig McGregor as:

Hundreds of thousands of red-brick bungalows with liver-colored tile roofs, mass-produced weatherboard houses, fibro cottages with galvanized iron roofs, each set in its own block of land with a lawn out the front and a garden out the back and perhaps a garage along the side, with a picket of brick fence to divide Emoh Ruo from the nature strip and a two-meter paling fence to give some privacy from the Joneses, a motor mower in the laundry, a goblin or kookaburra perched next to the front step, musical door chimes and a street number decorated with a Mexican asleep under his sombrero.

Notwithstanding suburban conformity, Sydney has at least shaken off the unkind title of "the world's smallest large city" — a gibe aimed at the alleged insularity of its citizens. Overseas travel has made many Sydneysiders realize that their city possesses in full measure the mixture of ingredients that distinguish great metropolises — a homegrown popular culture, a cosmopolitan population and, alas, organized crime. In recent years, the common talk both in and out of Australia has been that Sydney has suddenly "taken off" by joining the exclusive circle of world centers that are magnets for entrepreneurial energy, high finance and artistic talent.

Separated from Sydney by 540 miles of asphalt road and a well-established sense of rivalry, the capital of Victoria, Melbourne, has the reputation of being more staid than Sydney, more "English." Billy Graham, the American evangelist, said that Melbourne was the most moral city he had ever visited. A less flattering view was expressed by American actress Ava Gardner, who spent several months in Melbourne shooting the 1959 movie *On the Beach,* about the aftereffects of a nuclear holocaust. She said that it was "a good place to make a film about the end of the world in."

In fact, Melbourne's wide, straight streets, handsome 19th-century buildings and large area of parkland that fringe the central area of skyscrapers give it an air of gentility lacking in Sydney, and its network of electric trolleys seems pleasantly anachronistic. The city's strait-laced reputation stems less from the urban environment, however, than from its image as the home of the Australian establishment. From 1901 until 1927, when Canberra became the national capital, it temporarily served as the seat of government. Some federal offices still carry out their functions from Melbourne, and the city remains the headquarters of Australia's main political parties.

Melbourne is more culture-conscious than other Australian cities, housing the nation's leading art gallery — a reputation threatened by the new National Gallery in Canberra — and most of the small but serious literary and political journals. It is a traditional haunt of Catholic intellectuals and left-wing radicals. It has lovely pubs, and a night life that is centered on discotheques, rock-music clubs and eating out, often in BYOG ("Bring Your Own Grog") restaurants. In the 1970s, it was the home of experimental theaters, such as La Mama's and the Pram Factory, that spawned a new wave of Australian playwrights. More importantly

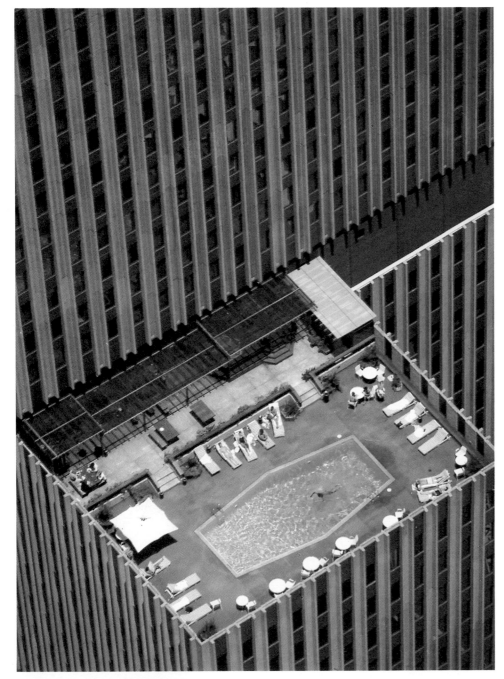

Guests at the colossal Hilton Hotel in Sydney's city center take their ease around a lofty rooftop swimming pool. The building boom of the 1960s and 1970s changed the character of the central districts of most of Australia's major cities, with the advent of high-rise office buildings and hotels.

for most Melburnians, the city is also the main focus of the nation's own brand of soccer, the 18-on-a-side Australian Rules, and the scene of the sport's Grand Final, an event that brings Melbourne to a virtual halt for one weekend each September.

Melbourne's image as a bastion of Anglo-Saxon culture is somewhat diminished by the fact that it is home to more immigrants than any other Australian city; its Greek ethnic population alone exceeds 125,000. At one of Melbourne's high schools, 90 percent of the 1,100 students have immigrant backgrounds, and a single high-rise apartment complex houses people who, among them, speak a total of 24 different languages. Partly in response to its large immigrant population, Melbourne is very socially aware; the city has a much wider infrastructure of community groups that serve the young, the unemployed and other minorities than Sydney.

Brisbane, Australia's third-largest city and the capital of Queensland, is less self-important than either Sydney or Melbourne. It has been called the best-acclimatized Australian city — a place with its shirt sleeves rolled up, as befits its semitropical setting. Its atmosphere is companionable, easygoing, hospitable, and a little rough around the edges. Even its traditional domestic architecture seems more appropriately Australian than that found in the other cities — wooden houses with verandas, raised on stilts to allow cooling air to circulate underneath. The picture has changed in recent years, however. The center of Brisbane is now skyscraper-modern, and the stilt houses that still remain are sought after by wealthy young couples trying to escape from the alternative accommodation of five-

COPING WITH THE SCORCHING SUN

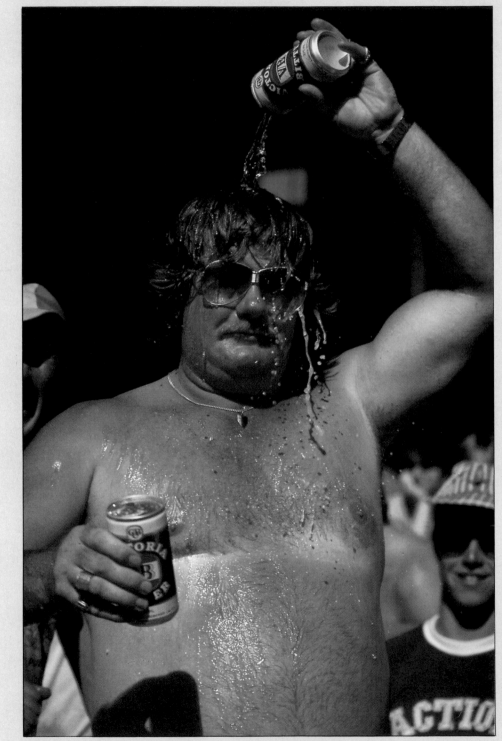

Australians' methods of reconciling the prevailing heat with their predominantly industrious and urban life result in a relaxed style that has become one of the defining characteristics of the nation. The continent's climate ranges from tropical in the far north to cool and temperate in Tasmania. Most of the population, however, is concentrated in the big cities, where average temperatures range from 57° to 68° F., and there is a reliable five or more hours of sunshine every day. The hottest months are from November to February, when temperatures of 80° F. are common in all the major cities except Hobart.

City dwellers react to the heat with some beguiling eccentricities. Some of these are customs in their own right, like the abbreviated uniform adopted by businessmen, who wear shorts and a shirt with a tie and street shoes; but others are the improvised tricks of individuals trying to keep cool according to their own ingenuity.

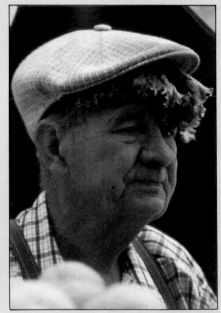

Beer is applied externally to cool one spectator at a cricket match.

A leafy frill shades a sidewalk vendor.

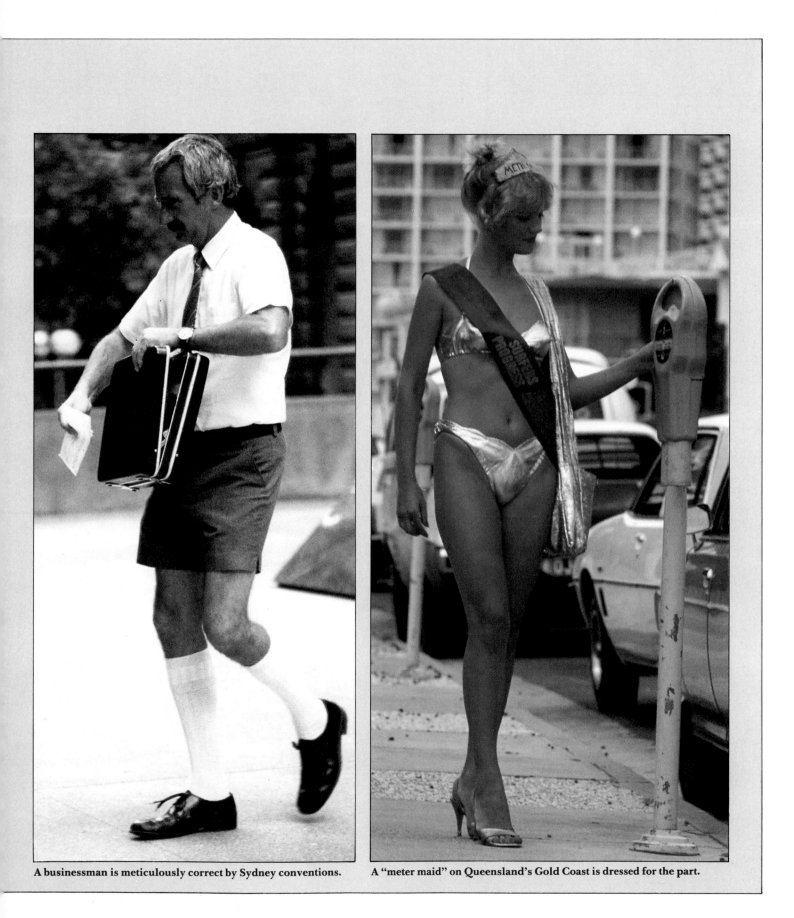

A businessman is meticulously correct by Sydney conventions. A "meter maid" on Queensland's Gold Coast is dressed for the part.

1

room boxes. The city's reputation for friendliness has also been tarnished by the poor civil rights record of its state government, particularly with regard to Queensland's Aboriginals.

With a population of approximately one million, Adelaide, the state capital of South Australia, is a little smaller than Brisbane and very different in mood and layout. It is the best-planned of the Australian cities, with a conventional grid design of single-story stone bungalows surrounded by a green inner belt of fine parks. In the past, it had a reputation for restraint and careful conservatism. This mood, it is alleged, stemmed from the fact that the city is unique in not tracing its beginnings to a convict settlement; instead, it was founded by staunch Presbyterians, full of civic pride and high business ethics. Its traditional image is changing, though. A large-scale program of industrialization has attracted many migrant workers, and the biennial Adelaide Festival has achieved international recognition as a showplace of the arts. According to Donald Horne — a perceptive analyst of Australian society — Adelaide goes ahead, while Brisbane falls backward, Sydney falls apart and Melbourne moves forward to stay where it is.

Separated from the rest of urban Australia by several million square miles of desert, Perth, the capital of Western Australia, is the most isolated city of its size in the world. Perth's more than 900,000 people live some 1,800 miles away from their nearest metropolitan neighbors, in Adelaide. Not surprisingly, the isolation at one time bred resentment among the inhabitants of Perth and Western Australia toward the wealthier states of the east. This resentment ran so deep that in 1933 Western Australia voted almost 3 to 1 to secede from the Commonwealth — a move vetoed by London. Since World War II, however, the massive mineral wealth of Western Australia has given the city an economic surge that none of the other state capitals can rival. And despite its isolation, Perth has acquired the reputation of being every Australian's second-favorite city, renowned for its pleasant blend of urban sophistication and relaxation. It boasts tree-lined streets, uncluttered suburbs and 520 square miles of parks, nature reserves and open spaces. It also has the Swan River as a focus for leisure and recreation. An estimated 1 out of 3 families have boats, giving it probably the highest proportion of yacht owners and small-craft proprietors of any large city in the world.

Most Australian cities grew haphazardly, but Canberra was planned from its conception. Although the Australian states federated in 1901, it was eight years before a suitable site was chosen for the new national capital. Unlike the other cities of the east coast, Canberra was to be located inland, on the western slopes of the Eastern Highlands, about 180 miles from Sydney and 400 miles from Melbourne. A worldwide competition to find a design for the city followed in 1911; a plan submitted by the American architect Walter Burley Griffin won. Another 16 years passed before enough of the city had been constructed for it to take over the duties of federal capital. And it was 40 years more before people took seriously the idea of living in the new capital, as opposed to working in it and going home to Sydney on weekends. With its formal squares, adorned by monumental public buildings, foreign embassies and statuary, Canberra still has the air of an administrative garrison town. It is a beautiful city — Australia's "pastoral symphony," as one writer fulsomely described it — that needs the addition of a yeastier population to leaven the mix of civil servants and administrators.

Hobart, the capital of Tasmania, was founded in 1803 with 433 residents, 281 of whom were convicts, and soon grew into a roistering whaling port. Since then it has grown bigger and quieter; as Donald Horne put it, "Hobart started life on the frontier and then went to sleep."

But nobody can seriously expect a city of about 170,000 people in a mainly agricultural, island state of fewer than 500,000 inhabitants to match the frenetic excitement of, say, Sydney — even though two of Australia's eight legal casinos are in Tasmania. Life in Hobart has been described as somewhere between small-town serenity and small-town vindictiveness; but then, that is a mainlander's attitude. Perhaps the kindest thing the rest of Australia can do is to leave the city as it is — sitting comfortably between the blue sea and the deeper blue mountains.

Despite being bombed by the Japanese in 1942 and being flattened twice by cyclones, Darwin — the capital of the Northern Territory — has not only survived but prospered, to become a clean, modern city of some 56,000 people. Whereas other Australian cities build high, Darwin builds long. Its buildings have few stories, to resist the cyclones that everybody knows will come again. Darwin's reputation for transience is perpetuated by a population of newcomers from other parts of Australia, as well as English, Greek, Chinese, Timorese, Lebanese, Vietnamese, Yugoslav and Italian immigrants — that makes the city look like a temporary cantonment for exiles in spite of its modern hotels and thriving casino. A sense of isolation and impermanence may be the root cause of its high rate of alcohol consumption — 40 percent higher than a national average that is itself one of the highest in the world.

Besides the dwellers in these capitals, another quarter of Australia's population lives in smaller towns based upon local industries — such as Newcastle, a coal port 60 miles north of Sydney; Broken Hill, a town of some 30,000 inhabitants that stands on top of what may be the world's richest silver, lead and zinc deposits; and Cairns, a tropical Queensland resort town of 40,000, built as the center of the local cattle and sugar industries, and now achieving importance as a big-game fishing center popular with well-heeled international sportsmen. A much smaller fraction of Australia's population is scattered in country townships. Parochial and old-fashioned, they often consist of a single main street flanked by clapboard houses that peter out into the surrounding bushland, and they seem to survive on dreams of their pioneering yesterdays.

Australia's far-flung population centers are linked by nearly one million miles of roads, of which about half are unsurfaced dirt tracks. Driving is more dangerous than in most other developed countries; the road-death rate is higher per capita than in comparable countries, such as the United States and Canada, and is twice as high as Britain's — a toll that is blamed primarily on drunk drivers.

The state-owned railroad system has suffered in the past from the fact that different lines used different gauges, so that until 1969 a journey from the east to the west coast involved at least

The look of the outback is illuminatingly interpreted in this 1890 painting of a bushman by Australian Arthur Streeton. Streeton was one of the first artists to portray the bush landscape without the romanticized conventions of European rural painting.

1

three transfers to different tracks. This situation is now being ameliorated by the introduction of a standard rail size. In any case, the continent is so large that, apart from short-range commuting, trains are the only suitable method of transportation for the leisured traveler or for bulk commodities, such as coal or agricultural produce. The journey from Melbourne to Perth still takes three days. The trip from Adelaide to Alice Springs normally takes slightly less time, though on at least one occasion the track was washed away by floods, and passengers had to be rescued by helicopter. The service is picturesquely nicknamed the Ghan — short for Afghan, from the nationality of the camel drivers who once provided the main competition for outback freight transport.

Most Australians traveling between the cities use the domestic air services. In the sparsely populated interior, aircraft not only carry travelers, but they also supply medical aid, through the celebrated Flying Doctor Service; they help to round up livestock; they seed and spray crops, and they deliver mail and library books.

Australians also keep in touch through a nationwide network of telephone, telegraph and postal services. Australian Telecommunications Commission is the country's biggest employer. Because of the enormous distances, services are — in theory, at least — tightly stretched. On the average, a post office serves an area of 440 square miles, and in thinly populated Western Australia, the figure rises to one for every 1,700 square miles.

Like the cities they inhabit, the Australian people have been changing over the past three or four decades, both in their make-up and in their self-image. The latter has in the past drawn heavily upon the bush and the tough, wiry, laconic characters supposed to inhabit it. In his penetrating study of the phenomenon, *The Australian Legend,* Australian historian Russel Ward has drawn a revealing portrait of the primitive Australian, beloved of brochure writers, sentimental politicians and film makers alike:

According to the myth the "typical Australian" is a practical man, rough and ready in his manners and quick to decry any appearance of affectation in others. He is a great improviser, ever willing to "have a go" at anything, but willing too to be content with a task done in a way that is "near enough." Though capable of great exertion in an emergency, he normally feels no impulse to work hard without good cause. He swears hard and consistently, gambles heavily and often, and drinks deeply on occasion. Though he is "the world's best confidence man," he is usually taciturn rather than talkative, one who endures stoically rather than one who acts busily. He is a "hard case," sceptical about the value of religion and of intellectual and cultural pursuits generally. He believes that Jack is not only as good as his master but, at least in principle, probably a good deal better, and so he is a great "knocker" of eminent people unless, as in the case of his sporting heroes, they are distinguished by physical prowess. He is a fiercely independent person who hates officiousness and authority, especially when these qualities are embodied in military officers and policemen. Yet he is very hospitable and, above all, will stick to his mates through thick and thin, even if he thinks they may be in the wrong.

The picture projected by this still-popular stereotype, as Ward goes on to say, grew out of the lifestyle of a tiny minority of the Australian population: the semi-itinerant workers — such as drovers, stockmen, station hands — all of whom earned their living in the outback in the late 19th and early 20th centuries. The values that the image enshrines are those of a rural proletariat, largely of ex-convict stock, for whom camaraderie, or "mateship" as the Australian version is usually known, was a necessity in the face of a hostile and alien environment. In short, it is a delineation of a class of people about as far removed as it is possible to be from the reality of most Australians' lives today.

Far from being the weather-beaten bushman of popular imagination, today's Australian belongs to the most urbanized large country on earth. Far from roaming rootlessly, he or she is more likely than his or her counterpart anywhere else in the world to be buying a house; the home-ownership figures are higher than 70 percent. The roving instincts of Australians are now largely confined to the young, who often travel overseas to "see the world" before they return home to settle down to careers and families.

Modern Australian society is predominantly middle class. As recently as 1961, there were almost as many blue-collar as white-collar workers in the country — about 1.5 million in each group — but since that time, the number of white-collar jobs has surged ahead. Between the 1961 and 1981 censuses, for example, the number of clerical workers rose by more than 500,000, and administrative, executive and managerial positions increased by 110,000. During the same period, the number of farmers and rural workers actually fell by 15,000.

The expansion of the white-collar population is linked to the growth of higher education. In 1939, there were 13,000 university students at six universities; by 1983, the figure had risen to 169,350 at 20 centers of learning. The demand for extra places had been fueled in part by a postwar baby boom that gave youth an increasing share of the nation's demographic profile. By the early 1980s, more than half the population was under the age of 30 and a third was under 20. It is not unreasonable to see in the lowering of the age curve one of the engines of the nation's current vitality.

Another fundamental demographic change has been the altering pattern of immigration. Up to the end of World War II, almost all immigrants came from the British Isles, reinforcing the Britishness of Australia's official institutions with their habits of thought and their social customs. New arrivals felt at home in a country where they could drive on the left and pay for things in pounds, shillings and pence (the Australian dollar dates only from 1966, when the currency was decimalized). The nation's institutions were equally close to those of the mother country. Not only did the laws strictly follow the British pattern, but judges wore the same anachronistic paraphernalia of robes and wigs. Children could be educated, if their parents wished, in private schools, and the universities were as British as their founders and staff could make them.

It was in the details of daily life, however, that the British flavor of pre-World War II Australia was most apparent. A culture that had evolved in a cold, wet, northern climate was thrown into high relief when imported lock, stock and barrel into the sunny light of the subtropical south. The work day in those times generally be-

gan at the same time it did in Britain: 9:00 a.m., when the sun was already blazing. Few people dared suggest that a Mediterranean timetable would be more comfortable, that it would make better sense to start in the cool of the morning and stop earlier — or else later, allowing for the restful interposition of a lunchtime siesta.

The clothes normally worn showed the same loyalty to ancestral conventions and disregard for comfort: dark suits with vests, collars and ties, "sensible" dresses. Eating habits were equally hidebound, focusing on incongruous, hot, meat-and-potatoes dinners. Such traditionalism reached its apotheosis at Christmas time, when

roast turkey and plum pudding were solemnly served in the best Dickensian manner in the sweltering heat of the high Australian summer.

Attitudes began to change in the course of the war. The shock of the Japanese threat, including the bombing of Darwin, led to a rethinking of attitudes that was to affect profoundly the structure of Australian society and ultimately to reduce the British influence. Politicians of every stripe came to the conclusion that the country was dangerously underpopulated and had insufficient forces to defend itself. A policy of assisting immigrants with the costs of passage was adopted, and it was extended to settlers from continental Europe as well as from Britain. The result was an influx of almost three million newcomers, arriving at an average rate of 100,000 a year, until restrictions were again imposed in late 1974. By that time, the proportion of Australians born overseas had doubled, from 1 in 10 to 1 in 5. Fewer than one third of the new arrivals came from Britain; Italy provided about 16 percent, Greece about 10 percent, with Germany and the Netherlands also contributing substantial numbers.

The most recent trend has been a large increase in the number of Asian immigrants. Since the 1950s, the infamous "White Australia" policy, used in effect to disbar Asian entry, has been gradually eroded. By the mid-1980s, roughly a third of all immigrants were Asian, and the "Asianization" of the country was an issue beginning to arouse political passions.

The changing structure of Australian society is reflected in the shifting pattern of religious allegiance. In 1933, nearly 40 percent of the population belonged to the Church of England, or Anglican Communion, and about 20 percent — mainly of Irish ancestry — were Roman Catholic; most of the remaining population was affiliated with other Protestant denominations. Yet by the mid-1980s, the number of Catholics — swollen by immigration from the Mediterranean countries — was rivaling the Anglican total, and about 3 percent of the population was Greek Orthodox. A growing number were churchless: Whereas in 1933 only one Australian in 500 claimed to have no religion, almost 10 percent of the population now had no religious allegiance.

Although tolerance prevails for the most part, Australia has had its share of religious discrimination. Until the 1960s, for instance, Jews were denied entrance to the Melbourne Stock Exchange, and Catholics were rarely granted admittance to the exclusive clubs that cater to the financial and farming élites. Polarization of a less harmful kind is also apparent in politics: Roman Catholics provide the backbone of support for the Australian Labor Party and, to an even greater extent, the Democratic Labor Party, a group that broke away from the ALP in 1956 over the issue of Communist infiltration of trade unions, which have traditionally been the ALP's chief backers. Conversely, Presbyterians and Methodists give strong support to the Liberal Party, the nation's main right-of-center grouping, and to the conservative National Country Party, the mouthpiece of rural voters. The country's other main political organization, the Australian Democrats Party, occupies the political middle ground and plays an important role in maintaining a balance between the parties of the right and left.

Religious differences also help account for the fact that in Australia, a country whose six states each operate a free public-education system, about one fifth of the primary schools and one quarter of the secondary schools are private, tuition-paying establishments. Some 80 percent of the private schools are Roman Catholic foundations. Most of the remainder are run on the English boarding-school model and are either Anglican or Presbyterian in their religious affiliation. In terms of the number of admissions to Australia's universities, these privately owned schools undoubtedly do better than the public schools.

Heated debates about the wisdom of giving Australians the choice between competing educational systems have not deterred recent immigrants from setting up their own private schools, dedicated to the preservation of minority cultures and languages. In fact, many of these establishments receive some funding from the government, reflecting Australia's shift away from a policy of assimilation and toward one of multiculturalism, or ethnic pluralism. In 1983, for example, Sydney's first full-time Greek school opened with an enrollment of 600 pupils and a three-year waiting list. In the same year, Australian Jews were operating 14 schools, including Victoria's Mount Scopus College, which has 2,300 students and is claimed to be the world's largest Jewish secondary school outside Israel. In 1983 there was also a full-time Spanish-language school in Canberra, a Japanese school near Sydney, a school in Sydney's western suburbs run by Hmong refugees from the mountains of Laos, and a gypsy school teaching Romany in Perth.

In appearance, then, the traditional view of the Australian as described by Russel Ward has long been consigned to the junkyard of legend. Yet, like many another cherished myth, it remains, in spite of all logic, unreasonably prevalent — so prevalent, indeed, that the observer ends up wondering whether, in spite of all evidence to the contrary, it might not still contain a grain of truth. Certainly, the realities of life in modern urban and suburban Australia hardly jibe with that tough, bushman image. Yet perhaps just through repetition and some deep desire in the national subconscious for the claim to be true, the picture retains a real force. Although the conditions that created the lifestyle have

DELICATE TRACERIES OF IRON

Houses in many hot countries are built with verandas and balconies to provide shade. In Australia's cities, however, these architectural devices are often given a special character by the traceried iron-work of which they are built.

In the mid-19th century, when Australian towns were expanding rapidly, iron was cheap and local taste ran to florid patterns. The gingerbread fussiness of typical 19th-century work later fell out of favor — indeed, in the 1940s many fine examples were destroyed — but the older districts of some cities, such as Paddington in Sydney and Melbourne's Carlton, still have buildings that strike a welcome note of frivolity among the usually utilitarian architecture.

Tracery embellishes a Queensland hotel.

A balcony on slender pillars casts lacy shadows on the walls of a house in Melbourne.

1

Wearing cadet uniforms for an Anzac Day parade, pupils at the prestigious King's School in Parramatta, Sydney, walk through its 300-acre grounds. Founded in 1832, King's is one of the more than 2,000 private institutions in Australia that account for about 20 percent of school enrollments.

disappeared, the approach to life it summarizes remains the most distinctively Australian feature of the continent's inhabitants to this day.

Australia began as a derivative culture, settled by Europeans centuries later than most of the New World, and it is still one today. Its bush is characterized by barbed wire and corrugated iron, products of the machine age of European civilization; its cities by skyscrapers and commercialism, products of the American age. The unique creation of Australian culture is to be found elsewhere: in a social ethos that, despite decades of affluence and high-pressure ways of thinking and living, has survived in modified form to the present day.

A large part of that ethic has to do with egalitarianism: the idea that every person should be, or at least act, equal. The English novelist D. H. Lawrence

noticed it when he came to Australia to write his novel *Kangaroo:* People there might feel "better off" than others but not "better," he wrote. Generations of immigrants from Britain and other status-conscious countries have commented on how informal and free from snobbery Australia appears to be.

This openness should not be confused with an absence of distinctions of class or wealth, which have been increasing with the nation's postwar affluence. But Australia remains determinedly democratic in its social conventions. Taxi drivers may still take offense if customers do not sit in the front of the car; tipping is less prevalent than in most Western countries; perfect strangers call one another "mate" and issue informal invitations to their homes. According to Donald Horne, writing in 1964, "If a Russian aristocrat of 1917 could see photographs

of Australia now, he might assume that it was here that the people had taken over, not Russia."

The Australian ethos also has something to do with character traits, such as friendliness. This is a modern descendant of "mateship," which was an exclusively male ritual; today you would have to add "sisterhood." Male and female, there is less of a sense of enclosure about the people than in, say, England or France or Sweden. On country roads in Australia people still nod or wave to each other when they pass, even if they are strangers. The same thing frequently happens on the beaches along the coast, or in town at bus stops or in elevators; it is an acknowledgement of commonality that is rare elsewhere in the world.

To understand Australia, the observer must search in the everyday habits of everyday people, for if ever there was a nation in which the pattern of life was dominated by the majority of the population rather than by a few individuals or an élite, it is Australia today. One reason for this lack of formality is the comparative brevity of white Australian history, which means that grand institutions and grand traditions have had less time to establish themselves than in older nations. Another factor is an Australian habit of "cutting the tall poppies down to size" — the tall poppies including anyone who is more successful than average — and in the words of the bush-balladeer Henry Lawson, making sure that the rich and powerful get "educated down." This tendency is less prevalent now, because Australia has become more status-conscious and competitive in the postwar years; but the social force of the common people remains formidable.

Finally, to come to terms with what

34

is most characteristic of Australian life, one must look outside the daily pattern of work. Work is not unimportant, but the general trends of employment — the shift away from the farm and toward the office, the movement of a large proportion of married women into the labor force — tend to be similar in most developed nations. It is what people do outside of working hours that most distinguishes one country from another, and in Australia leisure counts. There is an old, pervasive feeling that life is not made for work but for living. A South Pacific hedonism runs through the culture, tempting Brisbane office workers into the park for a longer-than-legal lunch of salad and beet sandwiches, luring truant schoolboys into the adults-only movie house in the Kings Cross district of Sydney, leading surfers to drift up and down the east coast in search of the unattainable perfect wave, drawing countercul-ture drop-outs to lead an imitation Aboriginal life in communes and cooperatives in the subtropical mountains to the north, and in colder Victoria bringing 100,000 roaring partisans to the Australian Rules Grand Final in the Melbourne Cricket Ground. All in their different ways are engaged in the time-honored pursuit of fun. Because a life of leisure, and not just for the leisure class, continues to be what much of the Australian dream is all about. □

The skeletons of hundreds of trees rise from the waters of Tasmania's Lake Gordon, swollen as a result of a huge hydroelectric project.

IMAGES OF AN ARCHAIC LAND

Australia is the driest and flattest of continents. Over great tracts of the interior — remote from the sea, desiccated and crumbled to dust by the relentlessly blazing sun — less than 10 inches of rain falls a year. Most of the lakes and rivers that appear on maps of these regions were formed in a long-past, wetter geological era and are now filled only by rare cloudbursts. During eons of geological silence, mountain ranges that once rose ruggedly from the plains have worn down to rounded stubs.

Yet no continent the size of Australia could fail to offer a variety of scenery. There may be few mountains that reach conspicuous heights, but rivers fed by the moisture-laden Pacific trade winds have cut dramatic gorges through the Great Dividing Range on the eastern seaboard. Farther south, in the cool, damp island state of Tasmania, lakes nestle between tree-clad slopes. Most spectacular of all, the nation's 22,041-mile shoreline boasts a catalogue of splendors, ranging from the surf-edged paradise of the southern beaches to the fantastical coral wilderness of the Great Barrier Reef off the Queensland coast.

In Tasmania's Central Highlands, a placid Lake Dove lies amid a forest of pine and eucalyptus beneath the twin peaks of Cradle Mountain. The deep lakes of the island state were gouged out 20,000 years ago — during the last ice age — when Tasmania was still joined to the mainland.

LAKES SUCKED DRY BY THE SUN

After rare rains, saline water fills South Australia's Lake Everard. It will soon evaporate, leaving a salt pan almost as parched as the sand dunes.

Dunes nicknamed the "Walls of China" border the bed of Lake Mungo in New South Wales, dry for 16,000 years.

THE UBIQUITOUS EUCALYPTUS

An avenue of hardy river gums, nourished by water stored in their leathery leaves, lines the dry bed of the Todd River near Alice Springs in the Northern Territory. The low rainfall of the outback ensures that the stream rarely flows.

Elegant karri trees, a type of
eucalyptus that can reach 250 feet,
tower over the verdant undergrowth of
the Warren River valley in the southwest corner of Western Australia.
Heavy rainfall and high humidity
make this the only area of the massive
state to support such dense vegetation.

The corrugated ridges of the Macdonnell Ranges run more than 200 miles across the Northern Territory, enclosing parallel valleys peppered with ghost gums — a kind of eucalyptus. These are among the oldest mountains on earth, eroded over 400 million years by the elements and old watercourses.

Dawn mist gathers in the valleys of the Blue Mountains, a section of the Great Dividing Range 60 miles west of Sydney. Rivers and streams have dissected this sandstone plateau to create a dramatic, fertile area of precipitous gorges, escarpments and peaks that are more than 3,000 feet high.

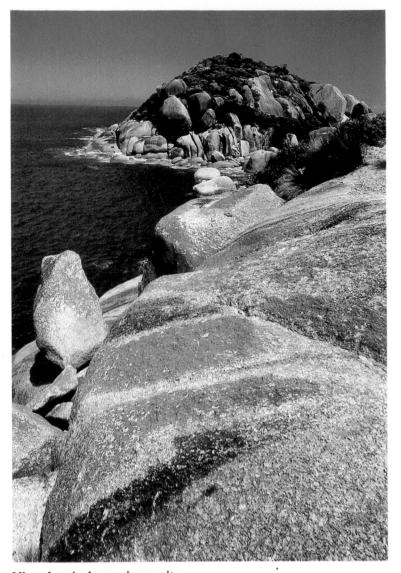

Minerals stain the massive granite boulders on Wilson's Promontory, the southernmost point of the Australian continent, 660 miles southeast of Melbourne. This rugged, hook-shaped headland, sculpted by sea and wind, was joined to Tasmania until the sea cut the bridge 8,000 years ago.

Motorboats stand off one of the innumerable sandy cays that, with larger atolls and islands, form the Great Barrier Reef. This 1,200-mile-long coral chain was created chiefly by the accumulation of the limestone casings of billions of polyps — tiny marine animals — over a period of 15,000 years.

COPYRIGHTED SEP 3 1888.   THE CITY OF SYDNE

EMERGING FROM A COLONIAL PAST

A print, made in 1888, shows Sydney 100 years after its foundation as a British penal colony. Possessing one of the world's finest harbors, the settlement quickly became a focus of trade and shipping, and by the time of its centennial, it had developed into a thriving metropolis of 350,000 people.

More than 35,000 years ago, the first settlers arrived in Australia. They came from Southeast Asia, and for the most part they walked. A great ice age had lowered the level of the oceans, and a fragile land bridge extended through what is now Indonesia and New Guinea to the empty southern continent. No one knows how long they spent on their journey, whether it was an epic or an ordeal, or whether they even knew that they were making it. Like every human at the time, they were hunter-gatherers, foraging in small bands; they may have fled in haste from violent neighbors or idly meandered after game and wild fruits, taking generations to make the crossing.

Then, many thousands of years after these wanderers arrived, the massive icecaps of the last glaciation thawed, and the waters rose once more. Tasmania was cut off from the Australian mainland, and of the great land bridge to Asia, only a scattering of islands, swept by perilous new seas, remained. For the people of Australia, a long age of peaceful isolation began.

Their continent, however, was not a paradise. The same climatic changes that had isolated it from the rest of the world had stricken much of this land with perpetual drought, and few areas offered an easy living. Like all hunter-gatherers, they were semi-nomadic and ranged over vast tracts of territory to make the most of a scanty food supply. They had few material possessions and used simple weapons: a stone-tipped wooden spear, for instance, or the curious throwing stick they called a boomerang. Except in the cooler, southern regions, they rarely troubled to make clothing.

Spiritually, though, their lives were rich and complex. Over the quiet, uncharted centuries, they developed an intricate web of totems and taboos that not only allowed them to harvest the frugal necessities of life from an often forbidding environment, but also provided intense inner satisfaction. Everything was magical; but it was usually a magic based upon acute observation of the natural world. Everything was part of the whole. A man could see his ancestors in a rock or a star, or in a kangaroo upon a far horizon. A whole people lived in a state of permanent communion with the world about them, transcending birth and death and time itself. That timeless lifestyle lasted for millennia and, left undisturbed, might have lasted for millennia more. But only distance and the ocean protected it; half a world away, in Europe, a very different kind of people, aggressive and ambitious, were finding how easily distance could be conquered.

Other peoples had perhaps probed toward Australia before the European explorers made their first landfalls. The Inca of Peru, for instance, told the Spanish invaders of a great expedition that they had made to a fascinating southern land. More probable is the

2

claim made by some modern Chinese historians that, in the sixth century B.C., their mariners had made the crossing from the Indonesian archipelago. A few fragments of Chinese ceramics — though of a much later date — have been found on Australia's northern coast. Macassar fishermen from Indonesia, in search of the delicacy known as *bêche-de-mer*, a form of large sea cucumber, are known to have been regular visitors. But the northern and northwestern shores, the most likely point of contact for venturesome Asian navigators, are unwelcoming. No permanent settlement was ever attempted in that area.

The European idea of a great southern continent can be traced back to the geographers of classical times, who theorized that an antipodes must exist to counterbalance the land mass of Eurasia. Since they also theorized that the equator was an impenetrable, fiery barrier, that seemed to be the end of the matter. Nevertheless, the idea of an unknown southern land, *terra australis incognita,* which was first proposed by the second-century Greek philosopher Ptolemy and then adopted by his Roman successors, continued to fascinate educated people. By the time the Portuguese launched the great age of exploration in the 15th century, the land's existence — although unproved — was more or less taken for granted.

The sea routes opened by the Portuguese around Africa to India and beyond made nonsense of the idea of an impassable equator. By the early 16th century, they were sailing and trading as far east as Java and mapping the northern coast of New Guinea. But despite tantalizing hints that they may have touched on the Australian mainland, there is still no firm evidence of

discovery. The wealth they brought back, however, encouraged others to explore the same far-off waters.

The Spanish made the next contribution. In 1606, Luis Váez de Torres traversed the dangerous shoals of the strait that now bears his name, passing south of New Guinea and within a few miles of the Australian coast. But Torres' feat went without public recognition for almost 150 years; fearful of competition from European rivals, the authorities in Madrid kept his report a closely guarded secret.

Their fear was understandable, because others were also at large in the

English explorer Captain James Cook *(left)* is seen in this portrait in 1776, shortly before the voyage that was to end with his death in Hawaii. Six years earlier, Cook had sailed his ship, *Endeavour (below)*, to the east coast of Australia, blazing a trail for British settlement there.

Pacific. In the same year that Torres completed his voyage, a Dutch ship under the command of Willem Janszoon, nosing around New Guinea in search of gold, made the first definite European landfall in Australia, on the desolate Cape York Peninsula.

The Dutch were traders par excellence, commercial leaders in Europe itself, and in the early 17th century, they were busily creating a lucrative mercantile empire based on Java. Unlike the Spaniards, they had no interest in glory: Their purpose was more mundane. An official of the Dutch East India Company, founded in 1602, declared: "With God's aid, we may obtain some great booty in the South Seas." Exploration was frowned upon unless the commercial benefits were clear. Almost despite themselves, the Dutch con-

trived to map nearly half the Australian coast, and they gave the continent its first European name, New Holland.

They were not very impressed by what they saw. Reports and ships' logs are almost unanimous: "In our judgment, this is the most arid and barren region that could be found anywhere on earth," wrote one captain in 1623; another, who was shipwrecked on the northwestern coast in 1629, declared the continent "an accursed earth."

Its inhabitants were even less appealing to the explorers. Abel Tasman, who between 1642 and 1644 had led two expeditions grudgingly financed by the company's merchants, called them "naked, beach-roving wretches, miserably poor." He said that they were "in many places of a very bad disposition." The English explorer-pirate William Dampier, who landed on the coast of northwest New Holland in 1688, was even more damning: "They have the most unpleasant looks and the worst features of any people that I ever saw, though I have seen great variety of savages."

No one recorded what the "savages" thought of their visitors: blotchy, white, scurvy-ridden, womenless men, with their floating islands of wood and cord and creaking canvas, their bizarre, sweat-soaked garments, their terrible weapons and their ignorant disdain of sacred places. Still, the interlopers were few in number, and in some of the early violent encounters it had been found that they could be killed. It would have taken a perceptive Aboriginal indeed to realize at the time that his people's long sway over their arid land, once counted in tens of thousands of years, would now be measured in decades.

For a while, however, it seemed as if the Europeans had gone away and forgotten all about them. The Dutch were

not interested in colonies, even if they had felt New Holland might support them; Spain and Portugal had enough to handle with their existing empires; and the rising powers of Britain and France spent much of the 17th and most of the 18th centuries at war with each other. Besides, the South Pacific was simply too far away, so the barrier of distance still held.

For more than a century after Tasman's voyages, the eastern coast of Australia remained unmapped. By the 1760s, though, both Britain and France were probing cautiously into the Pacific, partly lured by the old legends of *terra australis incognita,* partly inspired by the scientific curiosity of an age that prided itself on its enlightenment, and perhaps also, in Britain's case, influenced by the capture — during the Seven Years' War — of ancient Spanish and Portuguese charts of the area.

In 1770, Captain James Cook, the greatest Pacific navigator of all time, discovered the eastern shore. He mapped it with the painstaking accuracy for which he was famous, and he took back to Europe the first glowing report of the new land. Around the anchorage he named Botany Bay, after the variety of botanic specimens he found there, he reported "a deep black soil" that supported "as fine a meadow as ever was seen." Cook also put in the first good word for the land's people, despite the fact that they had greeted his arrival with a volley of spears. "They may appear to some to be the most wretched people on Earth," wrote the explorer, "but in reality they are far happier than we Europeans." Furthermore, he claimed that "they sleep as sound in a small hovel or even in the open as the King in his Palace on a Bed of Down." Nevertheless, as

49

2

was customary at the time, Cook did take possession of the eastern half of the continent, naming it New Wales to distinguish it from New Holland, far to the northwest.

Cook's reports were received with interest back home, but the British government could muster little enthusiasm for new colonies. The existing ones were trouble enough; in 1775, the long, nagging quarrel with the American colonies erupted into a full-scale war for independence, and Britain suffered one of her most humiliating defeats. The idea of risking the same kind of debacle in Cook's New Wales sent shudders down official spines.

Yet in the end, it was precisely the defeat in America that brought about the first white settlement in Australia. What was to be done with the American colonists who had remained loyal to the crown? Surely, pamphleteers argued, the British government owed them something, and what better way of repaying them than to settle them in the South Seas, where they would deservedly prosper, providing Britain with a bastion of power in the Pacific as well? In principle, the government agreed. But the British sympathizers were far away in America, and the government at home faced a problem more sordid and more pressing.

For more than a century, the 13 American colonies had served as a dumping ground for convicted British criminals. But the new United States would not have them, and since the beginning of the transatlantic war, the outcasts had been accumulating by the thousands in overcrowded prison ships anchored at Portsmouth and in the Thames River. Not only were the ships a menace to health, even by the standards of an unhygienic age, but every

The Australian flower *Erythrina vespertilio* was sketched by Sydney Parkinson, an artist who sailed with Captain Cook on his historic voyage of 1770. Parkinson died of typhoid on the journey home, and many of his botanical drawings were later colored in by an artist in England.

convict held there cost His Majesty the then-shocking sum of £27 per annum.

To money-conscious British bureaucrats, Australia began to seem like a promised land. Not only would it absorb the inmates of Britain's jails, but with a little luck, and taking Cook's survey reports at their most optimistic reading, an Australian settlement could provide the British Admiralty with a source of timber and other naval supplies. It could serve as a base for whaling in southern waters and as a port of call for Pacific traders, and it would discourage French naval activity in the region. If the convicts worked hard and rehabilitated themselves, so much the better. If not, they would be too far away to harm British society.

Orders were issued. In 1787, miserable and terrified convicts — 568 men,

191 women and 13 unfortunate children — were prodded, under armed guard, into the holds of 11 transports in Portsmouth harbor, and blacksmiths quickly chained them to the walls. On May 13, the convoy, complete with a retinue of seamen and of Royal Marines to guard the prisoners, set sail; and on January 18, 1788, the ships dropped anchor in the empty silence of Botany Bay. For most of the involuntary passengers, it seemed little cause for celebration. Nevertheless, that huddle of stinking transport ships was to be immortalized as Australia's First Fleet. The roaring of the anchor cables through the ships' hawseholes shattered the tranquillity of the bay; it also marked the end of a continent's long and peaceful sleep and announced the birth of a new nation.

It could scarcely have been born in less auspicious circumstances. The place did not match Cook's eulogies. Instead of the promised "meadows," the new arrivals found only a sandy wilderness. So unpromising was the original landing site in Botany Bay that within a few days the fleet moved on to the next harbor to the north, named Port Jackson by Cook but soon rechristened Sydney. The soil was better there, but even so, the task of cultivating the virgin land was a challenge to tax even an expert. And the convicts of the First Fleet were anything but expert.

It is a fond Australian myth that the nation's founders were a mixture of free-thinking political prisoners and stalwart poachers, who were condemned by brutal and repressive British laws. True, the laws were savage. Most of the convicts had been found guilty of offenses a more enlightened age would have regarded as trivial, and

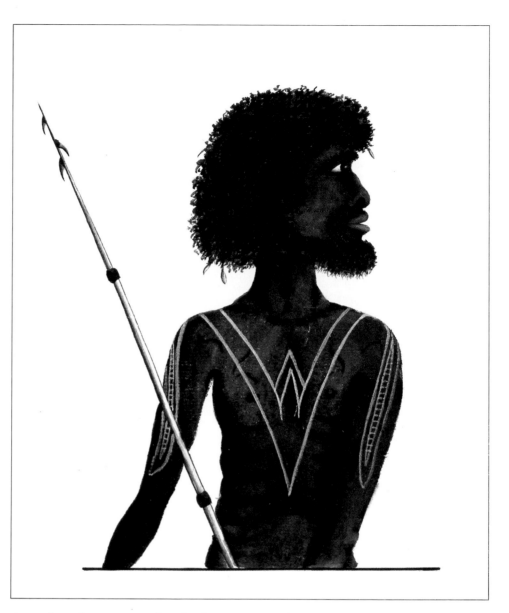

the colony's log book of their crimes, matched generally with a sentence of seven years' transportation, makes pathetic reading: "picking pockets"; "privately stealing"; "shoplifting"; or simply "misdemeanor." (Most of them were lucky to have escaped the hangman's rope.) But there were no political prisoners and very few poachers among them. The majority, in fact, were urban petty criminals, completely lacking in farming experience. And since they had been selected from Britain's crowded jails by officials eager to rid themselves of their most troublesome — or most useless — inmates, the convicts were unpromising material even for a force of unskilled laborers.

That the colony survived at all, let alone prospered, was largely thanks to one man, its governor, Captain Arthur Phillip. A regular naval officer, Phillip had already demonstrated his professional skills by bringing the First Fleet, intact and reasonably healthy, to Australia. Now he used skills of a different order, alternately bullying with the lash and cajoling with supplies of Royal Navy rum until some semblance of a settlement was created. But it was an uphill struggle. Even the colony's tools were "the worst that ever was seen," as Phillip wrote despairingly to London. And he got little help from the soldiers and the marines supposedly under his command. Their officers "declined any interference with the convicts" and lived as much as possible a separate existence. For two years, London ignored Phillip's complaints, and when, in 1790, the first ships from home appeared, they were carrying another batch of convicts to add to his troubles.

For the first few years, the colonists were almost entirely dependent on food supplied from overseas, and at times the colony was perilously close to starvation. Gradually, though, more and more land came under cultivation, and by the time ill-health forced Phillip's recall to England in 1792, the land now known as New South Wales was almost self-supporting. The first landowners were time-served soldiers and sailors, and convicts whose sentences had expired. They were granted title by the governor, who also used his power to create a new class of "emancipists" — convicts who were given a conditional pardon as a reward for good behavior. Emancipists were forbidden to return to England until their period of transportation was over; other than that, they were essentially free.

Slowly and painfully, they built the colony up. Sydney grew from a collection of crude huts to a scruffy but thriving little town, and isolated settlements sprang up in a hinterland that went as far as the Blue Mountains, which in the

2

early 19th century were regarded as an impassable barrier to westward expansion. Subsidiary convict settlements were built at Port Phillip, close to the modern city of Melbourne, in 1803 — a short-lived experiment — and in the following year at Hobart and Launceston in Van Diemen's Land, as Tasmania was known.

If free settlers were still reluctant to risk their futures so far from home, the British law courts continued to supply convicts aplenty. For the first time, they included a significant number of political offenders; in 1798 a failed rebellion in Ireland yielded about 1,200 embittered immigrants. Some of them staged another unsuccessful rising near Sydney in 1804; in the years to come, the Irish and their descendants would provide a noisily anti-British faction of the population, which helped to counterbalance misty-eyed sentiment about the mother country.

The most interesting early development, however, came not from the prisoners but from their guards. The New South Wales Corps was not, to put it mildly, the most distinguished unit in the British Army. But after a couple of years, its members began to show a remarkable commercial acumen. They realized their pay amounted to most of the colony's money supply, and they used their power to create an unbreakable trading monopoly — especially in rum, for which demand always exceeded supply. Soon they were able to transfer their profits into land, radically altering the future shape of the colony.

Originally, the plan had been to develop a self-supporting society: Free settlers and emancipists were to receive small grants of land and to be left on their own. But the land was poor, and so were its new owners. Unable to im-

Shown in a 19th-century illustration, British convicts sail in cages to far-off Australia *(top)*. Such shipments continued from 1787 to 1868, by which time 160,000 men, women and children had been transported. As the sample "passenger list" *(above)* shows, even shoplifting could lead to exile.

Entitled "The Landing of our Forefathers," an 1888 cartoon shows the British lion dumping prisoners ashore at Botany Bay 100 years earlier. Although convicts were soon outnumbered by immigrants, it was many years before the nation overcame its sensitivity about its origin.

prove it, or even to buy the livestock that could provide essential manure, they soon went bankrupt and sold out to the officers, who thus acquired large and reasonably profitable estates. The concentration of land and wealth increased even more when sheep were introduced, first for their meat and then, more lucrative still, for their wool. And when a governor — Captain William Bligh, victim of the *Bounty* mutiny of 1789 — tried to halt the process, his officers arrested and deposed him in 1808 for "tyranny." It seemed likely that the Australia of the future would be a country ruled by a tiny minority of powerful landowners, dominating a landless, poverty-stricken population.

But such a fate was not to be. The home government, finally shocked into action by Bligh's sequestration, sent an energetic new governor, Lachlan Macquarie, with a regiment of fighting men, and the New South Wales Corps was disbanded. Under the new regime, prosperity grew. Enterprising seamen, many of them ex-convicts, won wealth from sealing and whaling.

Nor was the little, settled strip of New South Wales any longer the extent of Australia. In 1813, the Blue Mountains were crossed for the first time, and excited explorers returned with tales of endless good grazing lands. Just as important, there were enough colonists to settle them. As late as 1820, there were still only 1,307 free immigrants; but reports were reaching London of emancipists who had made huge fortunes and been accepted by Macquarie as rehabilitated citizens, and Australia was at last being considered as a good place to send Britain's excess population, as well as its criminals.

Nor were the newcomers restricted to New South Wales. In 1829, Britain,

which had formerly laid claim to only the eastern half of Australia, extended its dominion to the entire continent, to preempt European rivals with an interest in the area. New settlements were springing up. Another penal colony had been established on the Brisbane River about 600 miles north of Sydney in 1824. The first settlement without convicts was founded near present-day Perth, in Western Australia, in 1829, followed by a colony near Melbourne in 1835. When Adelaide followed suit in 1836, all six capitals of today's states were in rudimentary existence.

All of these communities were on or near the coast, so that they could receive supplies by water. The opening up of the interior of the continent was a

more challenging matter altogether, and it fell to a courageous band of adventurers to make the pioneering journeys on which all further expansion depended. As early as 1829, Charles Sturt had set off from Sydney in an attempt to trace the southern river system to a hoped-for inland sea. The sea turned out to be illusory, but Sturt did discover enough good land to encourage the subsequent development of South Australia. A Scottish officer, Major Thomas Mitchell, discovered another vast area of good land in southeastern Australia in 1836. Christened Australia Felix by its discoverer, it was to be the nucleus of the future state of Victoria.

Less fortunate was 25-year-old Edward Eyre. In 1840, he discovered the

CHRONOLOGY OF KEY EVENTS

c. 35,000 B.C. The earliest Aboriginals appear in Australia, arriving across a land bridge from Southeast Asia. For thousands of generations, the Aboriginals live a finely balanced hunter-gatherer's life, dispersed in family groups over the continent.

1606 Willem Janszoon, a Dutch mariner, sails into the Gulf of Carpentaria, becoming the first European to land on the continent. In the next 30 years, Dutch navigators manage to chart much of the northern and western coastline, naming the territory New Holland.

1642 Dutch explorer Abel Tasman reaches Tasmania, mistaking it for the southern coastline of New Holland.

1770 Captain James Cook, the British explorer, lands in Botany Bay (now part of Sydney). He claims the whole eastern seaboard of Australia for Britain, naming it New Wales.

1788 Given the task of establishing a penal colony by the British government, Captain Arthur Phillip *(above)*, in command of the First Fleet, arrives with about 1,000 settlers, more than half of them convicts. Attracted by the safe anchorage and fresh-water stream, he establishes a settlement at Port Jackson — later named Sydney after Britain's then home secretary — near Botany Bay.

1793 The first independent settlers arrive to join the colony.

1797 John Macarthur, a lieutenant in the New South Wales Corps, introduces Spanish merino sheep, helping to lay the foundation of the future wool industry.

1798 A British expedition led by George Bass and Matthew Flinders circumnavigates Tasmania, showing it to be an island.

1801-1804 Matthew Flinders charts the coast of the mainland, establishing that the land is a single continent. He recommends its name be changed from New Holland to Australia.

1804 Hobart in Tasmania is founded as a new penal colony.

1813 An expedition led by the journalist W. C. Wentworth pioneers a route across the Blue Mountains, east of Sydney, opening up the continent's interior to settlement.

1817 Australia is officially adopted as the name of the continent.

1824 A penal settlement is founded at Brisbane.

1829 Perth is established in Western Australia by free settlers.

1835 Settlers establish themselves on the site of the future Melbourne, where a penal colony had previously failed to survive.

1836 Free settlers found the town of Adelaide.

1840 Transportation of convicts to New South Wales ends.

1842 Copper deposits are discovered and mined in South Australia *(below)*.

1850 The first Australian university is founded in Sydney.

1851 Gold is discovered, first at Bathurst in New South Wales, then in larger quantities at Ballarat and Bendigo in Victoria.

1854 The battle of Eureka Stockade — the only armed conflict to take place on Australian soil — pits miners against police and troops.

1855 The colonies of New South Wales, Victoria, South Australia and Tasmania are given self-government on local issues.

1859 Queensland is separated from New South Wales and given a similar constitution.

1860 Robert O'Hara Burke and William John Wills *(above)* make the first overland crossing of the continent, but they die on the return journey.

1862 John McDouall Stuart completes the first successful round-trip transcontinental crossing, from Adelaide to Darwin.

1868 Transportation of convicts to Australia finally ceases.

1872 Victoria becomes the first state to introduce free, compulsory, public education.

1876 Truganini, the last Tasmanian Aboriginal, dies.

1880 Ned Kelly, the most famous of the bushrangers (outback brigands), is captured and executed.

1890 Western Australia is granted self-government on local matters.

1891 The Australian Labor Party is formed.

1901 On January 1, the Commonwealth of Australia is proclaimed in Sydney, federating the six separate colonies — redesignated states — into an Australian nation. The future King George V opens the federal parliament in Melbourne *(below)*. A restrictive immigration law, effectively preventing most Asians from entering Australia, heralds the "White Australia" policy.

1902 Australia extends political suffrage to women, becoming the second nation in the world, after New Zealand, to do so.

1905 The Australian steel industry originates with the building of a blast furnace in New South Wales.

1909 Compulsory military training is introduced by act of parliament.

1914-1918 World War I inflicts 226,000 Australian casualties, including 60,000 killed, from a force of some 400,000 men — all volunteers, because two referendums had rejected compulsory conscription.

1915 On April 25, the Australian and New Zealand Army Corps (ANZAC)

participate with great heroism in Allied landings at Gallipoli. Anzac Day *(monument, below)* is to become Australia's foremost day of national remembrance.

1919 The League of Nations gives Australia a mandate over the former German colony of New Guinea.

1927 The national capital is transferred to Canberra.

1928 The Flying Doctor Service is established.

1939 With the declaration of World War II, Australia enters the conflict, fighting at Britain's side.

1942 Singapore falls to the Japanese, and 15,000 Australians become prisoners of war. Japanese bombing raids severely damage Darwin.

1945 Australian forces participate in successful attacks on Borneo. The war ends with 30,000 Australians dead and 65,000 wounded.

1951 Australia, New Zealand and the United States join in the ANZUS Pact, promising mutual assistance in case of attack.

1954 Australia joins the Southeast Asia Treaty Organization (SEATO).

1961 Oil is discovered in commercial quantities at Moonie in Queensland's Surat Basin, marking the start of the mineral boom of the following decade.

1962 The federal parliament gives adult Aboriginals the right to vote.

1965 An Australian military contingent (reaching 8,000 men by 1967) is sent to fight beside the U.S. armed forces in Vietnam.

1971 Australia brings back most of her troops from Vietnam, completing the withdrawal in 1972.

1973 Sydney Opera House *(below)* is completed.

1975 A constitutional crisis occurs in which Gough Whitlam, the first Labor Prime Minister in 23 years, is dismissed by Governor General Sir John Kerr.

1984 "Advance Australia Fair" replaces "God Save the Queen" as Australia's national anthem.

2

great salt lake that now bears his name, but then he marched, mostly alone, 900 miles along the coastal fringe of the barren Nullarbor Plain. He found only sun-baked, waterless wilderness, setting a pattern of disappointment repeated by most of his successors.

The population and economy of Australia were expanding at the same time as knowledge of the country's geography was growing. New settlers were arriving in floods. A total of 65,000 free immigrants landed between 1831 and 1840, at last outnumbering and eventually replacing the convicts. Many of the newcomers sought their fortunes in the thriving wool trade, and export figures matched the population rise: from less than 176,000 pounds in 1821 to more than

9.9 million pounds in 1840. For a time, the New South Wales government, worried about the likely effects of uncontrolled development on the colony, attempted to restrict any outward expansion. Land grants ceased and a system of purchase took their place (the proceeds were used to subsidize emigration from Britain); in 1829, settlement outside the "nineteen counties" around Sydney was declared illegal.

But no one paid much attention. If a man could not be a landholder, he would be a squatter, driving his herd of sheep — often bought on credit — into the virgin wilderness and establishing his "run." The word "squatter" had once been a term of abuse directed at vagrants; now, however, it described a way of life that attracted some of the

colony's most venturesome spirits, and the name became a title borne with pride. In 1836, the government relented, granting official squatters licences for the interior.

Many squatters made huge fortunes (in time, the term "squattocracy" was coined to describe them), but their life was never easy. With a few unskilled shepherds, usually convicts, they used to set off for the middle of nowhere with their flocks of sheep and hope for a good increase. Drought, incompetence and sheer bad luck — not to mention the alarming fluctuations in the international wool market — caused many bankruptcies. As one squatter with a taste for wry verse wrote:

Of sheep I got a famous lot —
Some died of hunger, some of rot,

——— STURT 1829-1830	
——— MITCHELL 1836	- - - LEICHHARDT 1848
——— EYRE 1840-1841	——— STURT 1859-1862
- - - STURT 1844-1845	——— BURKE AND WILLS 1860-1861
——— LEICHHARDT 1844-1845	——— GILES 1875

The map at left traces the routes taken by some of Australia's early explorers. One of the greatest was Charles Sturt, who navigated the river system from Sydney to the south coast in 1829 — a journey of more than 800 miles. Spurred on by his success, Sturt planned an even more ambitious expe-

For the devil a drop of rain they got
In this flourishing land of Australia.

The squatter lifestyle was not an existence that appealed to everyone, and a majority of the new immigrants chose to remain in the towns. Of the total Australian population, 40 percent was concentrated in the six cities, especially Sydney, as early as 1850. Indeed, after 1840, when the British government discontinued the practice of transporting convicts to New South Wales, the squatters were faced with an increasing labor shortage.

Colonial life was beginning to settle into a prosperous and regular pattern when Australia was suddenly thrown into the greatest — and also the least expected — upheaval in its short history. In 1851, gold was discovered at Bathurst in New South Wales and then, a few months later, at Ballarat, only 60 miles from Melbourne in the recently separated colony of Victoria.

The colonial establishment looked on the finds with horror. The *Sydney Morning Herald* predicted "calamities far more terrible than earthquakes or pestilence," while the *Bathurst Free Press*, closer to the scene of the action, declared that "a complete mental madness appears to have seized every member of the community." They had a point. Virtually overnight, Australian cities emptied in a fortune-hunting stampede, and as word spread round the world, boatloads of eager new immigrants jammed Australian ports.

The people came from every social class. "There were merchants, cabmen, magistrates and convicts," wrote one observer, "amateur gentlemen, fashionable hairdressers and tailors, cooks, coachmen and lawyers' clerks and their masters, doctors of physics and music, aldermen, scavengers, sailors, a real live lord on his travels — all leveled by community of pursuit and of costume."

The myth of the squatters was joined by the myth of the "diggers," as the prospectors came to be called — another comradely group, hard-bitten perhaps, but democratic to the core. Like all good myths, at heart it contained truth. Historians still argue over the extent to which the diggers transformed Australian society; most agree that they merely accelerated a process of growth that was already under way.

dition, and in 1844, crowds gathered in Adelaide *(above)* to watch as he set off in search of an inland sea that he believed lay at the continent's heart. The sea proved to be a myth, however, and after months of trudging through desert, Sturt returned home, his health broken and his dream shattered.

2

Certainly, the gold fields brought immense wealth to the colonies. At peak production, the Victoria fields yielded approximately one third of the world's supply. Their most important contribution, though, was not be to measured in precious metal, but in the people who came to seek it. Successful or otherwise, most of the adventurers stayed on. In 10 years, the population of the country tripled, and it became obvious that Australia was no longer a colonial backwater to be administered from London for the convenience of the British government.

Even before the gold rush, Australians, especially the squatters, had agitated for representative government, and in the course of the 1840s, they had won a steadily increasing say in their own destiny. But the powers of the colonial legislative councils were restricted, and so was the right to vote. Given the huge rise in population, it was not a situation likely to promote stability.

In 1854, the gold miners — excluded, like most Australians, from the franchise — gave a warning of the sort of troubles that might be in store. Generally, the gold diggers were remarkably peaceable, and most observers of the Australian fields agreed that there was little of the general mayhem and murder associated with the Califonia gold rush of 1849. But after three years' intensive panning, the easiest pickings were gone — and with them went the good temper of those who had yet to make their fortunes. When the governor of Victoria raised license fees and enforced his decision with a brutal and incompetent police force, one group of miners took to arms. As an act of defiance, they fortified a hill at Eureka, near Ballarat, and demanded reforms that included full manhood suffrage.

The authorities, acting quickly, used police and troops to storm the place: More than 20 men died.

The incident was little more than a riot, provoked by genuine grievances and repressed violently by a panicky government. The trouble never spread, and there were no martyrs, probably because the people killed in the fighting included policemen. Although the ringleaders were formally arraigned for high treason, all of them were acquitted. The miners' complaints — which mostly concerned the daily administration of the fields — were soon rectified, and it is likely that conditions would have improved even without the Eureka Stockade. As for manhood suffrage, when it was granted shortly afterward, only a minority of the diggers bothered to vote.

For nations, though, legends are often more important than fact, and symbols can carry far more power than dull reality. The image of those dusty, democratic diggers in the hot Ballarat summer, standing up for their rights against the oppressive might of the British Empire, has a permanent place in the Australian imagination. Mark Twain called it "the finest thing in Australian history," and references to the stockade as the birthplace of Australian democracy are common.

But perhaps the greatest significance of the episode is negative: It never happened again. Compared with other nations, old and new, the internal history of Australia is blessedly uneventful. The nation was built with sweat, not with blood.

By the end of the 1850s, five Australian colonies — New South Wales, Victoria, Tasmania, South Australia and the newly created Queensland — governed themselves on local issues, although London still controlled defense and foreign policy. Transportation was a thing of the past. The squatters might look back nostalgically to the cheap labor it had provided, but most other Australians were anxious to sell their own labor for the highest possible price and saw the convicts as unfair competition. In addition, convicts offended the rising national pride. There was, however, one ironic exception: The colony in Western Australia, founded exclusively as a free settlement, was in such dire straits by the 1840s that its landowners successfully petitioned London for convicts. Despite loud criticism from the other colonies, transportation in the west continued until 1868; the use of convicts is part of the reason that Western Australia did not achieve self-government until 1890.

If the colonies were becoming increasingly independent of Britain, they were even more independent of one another. The problems each faced were similar. The assemblies spent much of their time wrangling over systems of land allocation, and each colony suffered from the cycles of economic boom-and-bust that overlaid and sometimes masked their steady progress. But they tried to solve their problems individually, adding walls of tariffs to the barriers of distance that already divided them.

Of course, variations in the continent's climate imposed some differences between them. Queensland, for example, with its tropical northeast, devoted much effort to the cultivation of sugar cane. Plantations followed the pattern of the American South rather than the Australian south, and to work them, the sugar planters imported Polynesians — known as Kanakas, from the Hawaiian word for "person" — under a bonded labor system that to the other colonies looked suspiciously like slavery. Faced with opposition from a clamorous labor movement in southern Queensland as well as from elsewhere, the northern planters attempted to secede. But the British government would have none of it, and the problem remained unresolved beyond the turn of the century.

One factor common to Australians in all the nascent states was a growing fascination with the still-unexplored interior of their own continent. Charles Sturt, one of the pioneers of inland voyaging, set off again in 1844, this time north from Adelaide, carrying a portable boat that he planned to sail on the fabled inland sea. He got as far as the Simpson Desert before hunger, thirst and illness drove his party back. A German immigrant, Ludwig Leichhardt, had better luck. Also in 1844, he set off on a year-long trek northwest from Brisbane; he discovered many tracts of good grazing land, before finally arriving at Port Essington, a short-lived settlement 100 miles east of present-day Darwin, in the far north of the continent. But a second expedition revealed Leichhardt to be an incompetent organizer, and on his third, in 1848, he disappeared without a trace in the central void — a tragedy that provided the 20th-century Australian author Patrick White with a theme for his epic novel, *Voss*.

Exploration fever reached its climax in 1860, when the South Australian government offered a handsome cash reward for the first south-north crossing of the continent. Two very different expeditions strove for the prize. The first party to reach the north coast was led by a hot-headed Irishman called Robert O'Hara Burke; but a combination of bad luck and bad judgment prevented Burke and his partner, William John Wills, from returning alive. The credit for achieving the first two-way crossing was to go to Burke's methodical rival, the Scotsman John McDouall Stuart, who made the return trip on his third attempt in 1862.

After Stuart's trip, even the most fervent of optimists gave up hoping for

2

the cherished inland sea, and no one was surprised when the heroic east-west crossing of the continent by Ernest Giles in 1875 simply confirmed the bad news: Australia's heart was a scorched, stony wasteland. The vast Northern Territory would remain a useless desert. To the increasingly urbanized Australian population, living in the increasingly comfortable coastal cities, the bleak discoveries made little difference. But at least the explorers' tales found an eager audience. Few of the city dwellers would ever see the outback, or "bush" as it was called, but for all of them, it was becoming an essential part of their new Australian identity.

And if the wide-open spaces themselves were not enough, they also gave the Australian folklore its most popular characters — the bushrangers. Originally, these had been escaped convicts and other desperadoes who made a living by armed robbery on the fringes of the settled areas. In Tasmania at one time they had been a real menace. The gold rush had greatly expanded their opportunities and their numbers, to the extent that the mail coaches serving the gold fields rarely traveled without armed escort. In the circumstances of the 1870s, the bushrangers took on a new role, that of Robin Hood, supposedly robbing the rich to help the poor. In fact, they robbed whomever they could, and there are no recorded instances of their acting as a welfare agency. But sensational reports of their exploits thrilled city people, and the rural poor were happy to see wealthy squatters suffer from the bushrangers' attacks. Bad roads and a much-hated police force were the bushrangers' greatest allies, and when communications improved, the profession inevitably became obsolete.

Still, they had an undeniable appeal. When Ned Kelly, the most celebrated of them all, was captured — in spite of a bizarre suit of armor he had fashioned to protect himself from police bullets — 32,000 people signed a petition urging clemency. But the authorities hanged him anyway, in 1880; within a few years, the telegraph and the railroad had made his legend as misty and far-off as that of Captain Phillip and the convict fleet.

The bushranger phenomenon was one symptom of the antiauthoritarian attitude of the Australian people. A far more important indication was the steady rise of a powerful labor movement. It had begun with the nervousness Australian workers felt at the competition offered by convict labor, and it was quick to claim the Eureka Stockade as an early battle honor. Labor's first notable achievement, however, was the forcing of Chinese immigrants to move from the gold fields, and by the time of the first intercolonial trade-union congress in 1879, one of its demands was for the establishment of a "White Australia" policy. That policy, once implemented, did not begin to crumble until a century later. Like the convicts before them, the Chinese were seen as a threat to the living standard of other Australian workers, and by the end of the 1850s, most city-based Australians had a high standard of living to defend. In the following decades, the unions consolidated their position, with an unheard-of eight-hour day in most industries and wage levels that were the envy of the working-class world.

It was not, by European standards, a socialist movement. A strong Irish-Catholic influence ensured a healthy respect for property and propriety, as well as a dogged militancy; and most of the other elements to be found in Australia's powerful trade unions shared a genuine pride in being part of the immense and successful British Empire. Workers were far less interested in building a new society than in carving themselves a healthy share of the society they already had. Only in the 1890s, when economic crisis shook every Australian colony and a campaign of nationwide strikes failed to keep wages high, did the labor movement seriously go into politics; but when it did, with the foundation of the Australian Labor Party in 1891, its candidates were soon being sent to state assemblies.

In time, labor candidates would be elected to more than state assemblies. The economic panics at the end of the 19th century finally pressured the six colonies into federation. The more perceptive politicians had been suggesting such a step for Australia for decades; and the imperial government in London, which had granted autonomy to a federal Canada as early as 1867, had no objection to the plan. Even so, negotiations — backed up by referendums in each state — took almost a decade. Constitutions were drawn up, haggled over, scrapped and then drawn up again. Not until the first day of 1901 did the Commonwealth of Australia come into existence.

The constitution set up by the Commonwealth Act of 1901, as passed by the British parliament, is still in force today. "The legislative power of the Commonwealth shall be vested in a Federal Parliament," runs Section I, "which shall consist of the Queen, the Senate and a House of Representatives." As the wording of this section suggests, what follows is in essence a skillful amalgam of the British and

Wearing a suit of homemade armor, the legendary outlaw and compulsive exhibitionist Ned Kelly fought his last battle with the police in 1880 *(below)*. A shot in the foot led to his capture. He was photographed *(left)* a few months later, before he was hanged.

the American systems of government.

The head of state is still the queen — in her capacity as queen of Australia, however, not as queen of Britain — and the signature of her representative, the governor general, is required for validation of any legislation. The governor is bound, by the same conventions that exist in Britain, to accept the advice of his or her ministers, but retains certain prerogatives, including the right — rarely used in practice — to dismiss governments.

The House of Representatives can be compared to the British House of Commons. Seats are apportioned nationwide according to population, and the House is responsible for initiating financial legislation. The prime minister and most of the cabinet are members, and elections take place at three-year intervals — although, as in Britain, the prime minister can call for a dissolution and a general election at any time during that period.

The Australian Senate is much more like its Washington model than the British House of Lords. Twelve senators are elected from each state (plus two each from the two Territories), regardless of population, for a six-year term; half come up for reelection every three years. As a result, the balance of parties is rarely the same in the Senate and the House, and since the Senate has a veto as well as an amending power over legislation, the constitution discourages radical change.

Power is additionally shared with the legislative assemblies of each individual state, which retain a great deal of autonomy — although, since the Commonwealth was created in 1901, the federal government has tended to increase its authority at the states' expense. As a rule, the states are responsible for education, transportation, law enforcement, health services and agriculture; but since the federal government has unlimited powers of taxation, it maintains tight control of the states' purse strings. In addition to the various elected assemblies, the constitution also provides for a system of supreme courts in each state, as well as the High Court of Australia, which handles both appeals from the states and strictly federal matters. Like the United States Supreme Court, the High Court can rule — and frequently has ruled — that legislation is unconstitutional and therefore void. The High Court will also disallow laws that extend federal powers into areas of state concern.

The constitution has been regarded, accurately, as a device for protecting "middle-class, property-owning conservatism"; but in terms of franchise, it has always been robustly democratic. By 1901, indeed, Australia had as long a history of broad-based democracy as any nation in the world; even as early as 1860, the secret ballot practiced in most Australian states was known to envious

Britons as the "Australian ballot." The Franchise Act of 1902 extended federal voting rights to all men and women over 21 — except for the Aboriginals, who had to wait another 60 years for the vote — and in 1925, perhaps fearful of the consequences of apathy, legislators made voting compulsory for all Australians. The act was amended again in 1974, when the voting age was lowered to 18.

Independent or not, the new Commonwealth was firmly part of the British Empire. The late 19th century had seen a considerable amount of anti-British grumbling, especially among the Irish-descended community. After federation, however, Australians seemed to settle down as the empire's most loyal citizens. The "White Australia" policy was rigorously enforced: Almost all of the Kanakas who had been brought to work in the Queensland sugar-cane fields were sent home in 1906 and 1907. Its mechanism was a dictation test that any would-be immigrant had to take. Learning English was not enough to guarantee success, for the test could be conducted in any European language. English-speaking Chinese, for instance, often found themselves confronted with an examination in Italian. Whatever the rights or wrongs of the policy, it was effective: Of a population under five million in 1914, more than 95 percent were of British descent.

In any case, Australia's attachment to the British Empire was by no means entirely sentimental. The continent was practically defenseless: Without the shield of Britain's Royal Navy, there was nothing — or so some alarmed Australians had been claiming for a generation — to guard it from the designs of rapacious European powers, not to mention the Asian nations just above the equator. In return for imperial protection, most Australians were content to pay their imperial dues — in loyalty, in financial contributions and, if the time came, in blood.

The outbreak of World War I took Australia by surprise, but the majority of its people supported Britain wholeheartedly and without any complaint. Although there was no direct threat to Australia itself, thousands of young men volunteered to fight for the empire at the opposite end of the earth. The British, to begin with, were skeptical of the likely worth of what many senior officers regarded as raw colonials; but the test of battle proved that the Anzacs — the Australian and New Zealand Army Corps — were among the finest fighting soldiers of the war. Without conscription (vetoed by a nationwide referendum), Australia mustered more than 400,000 troops — 11.2 percent of the total population.

They were an unconventional army, easygoing and egalitarian, frequently insubordinate and rarely properly dressed. In action, though, they were a devastating force. They had many admirers, among whom was the daughter of British Prime Minister Herbert Asquith. She wrote: "Their spirits and *élan vital* know no bounds and their physique and appearance are magnificent. Men like young gods, bare to the waist, burnt brown by the sun." But the young gods were not immortal. More than half of them were to be wounded in the fighting, and 60,000 of them never saw Australia again. They left their bones on almost every battlefield in France, in Palestine, in Syria and, above all, on the rocky little Turkish peninsula of Gallipoli.

It was at Gallipoli in 1915 that the Anzacs were blooded for the first time, in a daring invasion that was expected to lead to the capture of Constantinople and the elimination of Turkey from the war. In fact, it was a disaster. Despite horrifying casualties, the invaders never succeeded in gaining more than a few miles of ground, and in the end, the whole force was evacuated. Yet, for Australians, the heroism of the Anzacs transformed Gallipoli, their only wartime defeat, into a great moral victory. Their sacrifice was seen as conferring a new kind of mystic nationhood on the whole Australian people, their final coming of age. April 25, the anniversary of the landing, was celebrated as Australia's great national day, and even today, despite the passing of time and the debunking irreverence of Australia's young, the day still carries enormous significance.

After the war, Australia sank into torpor, suffering badly from the Great Depression, which crippled the world economy in the 1930s. The nation was still very much under Britain's imperial wing — as late as 1939, for example, Australia's only full diplomatic representation overseas was in London; diplomatic relations with the United States were handled by an Australian counselor attached to the British Embassy in Washington. In 1931, the British Parliament passed the Statute of Westminster, which conveyed unequivocal independence to the white dominions of the empire; far from being eagerly welcomed, the statute was received by Australians with some suspicion, and they did not even ratify it until 1942.

World War II changed the old imperial relationship irrevocably. In some ways, indeed, the conflict could be described as Australia's involuntary war of independence, although few fore-

Families in Liverpool wait to board a ship for Australia in 1913. Lured by the prospect of regular work, high wages and generous subsidies from state governments, 65,000 Britons annually emigrated to the continent in the years before World War I.

2

saw — and even fewer would have desired — such an outcome when the fighting began. Unlike 1914, Australia this time was in the front line. In World War I, convoys taking Anzac troops to Europe had been escorted by ships of the Imperial Japanese Navy, allied to Britain. In World War II, there was no such alliance: Britain's Far Eastern empire crumbled with terrifying speed before the onslaught of Japanese armies. Japanese troops invaded New Guinea. Japanese aircraft bombed Darwin. It was painfully clear that Britain — the bulk of her dwindling resources committed to a mortal battle in Europe against Nazi Germany — was no longer capable of affording the effortless imperial protection that Australians had taken for granted.

Under the pressure of events, the instinct for self-preservation proved far stonger than sentimental ties with the mother country. If Britain could not protect her, Australia would have to look elsewhere. In an epoch-making speech at the end of 1941, Prime Minister John Curtin declared: "Without inhibitions of any kind, I make it quite clear that Australia looks to America, free of any pangs as to our traditional links or kinship with the United Kingdom." He added, "We know that Australia can go and Britain can still hold on." He did not say, but clearly he had it in mind, that events might turn out the other way around.

Of course, both Britain and Australia did hold on. After the grim year of 1942, the Pacific war settled down into the slow and bloody process of expelling the Japanese from the territory they had so quickly conquered. But the Australia that emerged in 1945 was not the Australia that had gone to war in 1939, and the world in which it found

itself had changed even more profoundly. For one thing, the British Empire had all but vanished, and although it took another 20 years for the ink to dry on the imperial death certificate, it was clear that the future security of Australia lay in the nation's alliance with the United States.

Even more important, the explosion of independent Asian nations from the ruins of the prewar colonial empires vastly increased the complexity of the Pacific region and presented Australia with a great postwar dilemma. Was the country to remain an aloof, European outpost, or should it become an integral part of the new comity of developing nations? Was Australia's future to be one of apprehension or of enthusiasm — stagnation or opportunity?

It is only with the advantage of hindsight that 1945 is revealed as a historical watershed. At the time, neither the changes nor the choices were immediately apparent to anyone, and the most general popular feeling was a profound desire to get "back to normal." By normalcy, however, no one meant a return to the economic doldrums and high unemployment of the 1930s; in any case, wartime development — notably a vast increase in manufacturing industry, as the embattled nation had struggled to attain self-sufficiency — made such a prospect unlikely. The Australian people wanted peace and quiet — and, above all, prosperity.

After the first few unsettled postwar years, Australians seemed to find the answer to their prayers in the person of Robert — later Sir Robert — Menzies. As the head of a reformed but thoroughly conservative Liberal Party, he won electoral victory in 1949, and then remained Prime Minister — and, to all

intents and purposes, the personification of Australia both at home and abroad — for an astonishing 16 years. Menzies certainly delivered prosperity, and in terms of peace and quiet, his government introduced little in the way of dramatic new legislation — too little, his detractors claimed. Yet paradoxically, this most conservative of politicians — who proudly called himself the "Queen's man" and cherished the old imperial connection — presided over the most remarkable period of change in Australia's history.

The most startling, and perhaps the most permanent, alteration was in the composition of the Australian population. The long-standing "White Australia" policy came to an end, at least in its British-only sense, and immigrants flowed from continental Europe by the thousands. It was reckoned that more newcomers came to settle in Australia during Menzies' term of office than in the half century before World War I. The immigrants succeeded in injecting an element of cultural diversity and sheer vitality that many observers had found lacking in the staid and somewhat provincial Australian society of the prewar years.

In the postwar period, too, Australia began to discover for the first time the uncertain delights of a foreign policy at last independent of Great Britain. To some extent, it was simply a matter of confirming the change of mentors forced upon the nation by the war. The ANZUS Pact of 1951, a defense agreement between Australia, New Zealand and the United States that pointedly excluded Britain, was no more than a recognition of an altered balance of power. And Australians, for the most part, supported their new ally with the same loyalty they had previously given to

BRAVE SERVICE ON BATTLEFIELDS ABROAD

An Australian dispatch rider gallops past newly dug war graves at Gallipoli in 1915.

Fresh from campaigning in Syria, Australian forces parade through Beirut in 1941.

In 1966, Australian troops make their way past an ox-drawn wagon in Vietnam.

On January 1, 1901, the Commonwealth of Australia was born. Instead of being divided into six British colonies, the continent was now a nation in its own right — but a nation that chose to remain locked in the imperial embrace.

Loyalty to the British Empire was to dominate Australian thinking for much of the next half century. It found dramatic expression during World War I, when thousands of Australians volunteered to fight for king and empire.

Although lacking in parade-ground discipline, the Australians soon won a reputation for courage and endurance. Storming ashore on the Turkish peninsula of Gallipoli in 1915, they withstood murderous enemy fire for eight months and suffered 28,000 casualties before a withdrawal was ordered. By the end of the war, 330,000 Australians out of a population of fewer than five million people had seen active service overseas; nearly 60,000 had died.

With the outbreak of World War II, thousands of young Australians again flocked to the far-off battlefields of Greece and the Middle East. This time, however, the conflict would shatter rather than strengthen the old imperial ties. With the fall of Singapore to the Japanese in February of 1942, Australians had to face the fact that they could no longer depend on British naval power for the defense of their homeland.

After the war, they consequently sought to strengthen their ties with the one nation that they felt could guarantee their security — the United States. A measure of the depth of the new relationship was the decision of the Australian government to send troops to Vietnam in 1965. Once again, Australian forces — at one point numbering 8,000 troops — fought on foreign soil, but this time in response to developments on the Asian mainland to the north.

Wigged and gowned in the British manner, two barristers hurry along a Melbourne street on their way to the law
courts. Each state has its own hierarchy of
courts, whose proceedings and decisions
are modeled on England's legal system.

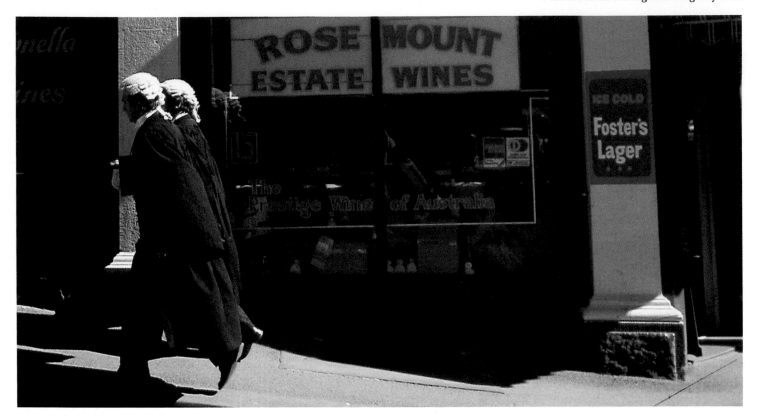

Britain. Australian troops were the first to join the Americans in Korea in 1950; more controversially, Australia was just as quick to send fighting units into Vietnam in the 1960s.

The controversy took a little time to emerge, however. When Menzies left office in 1966, it seemed for a while that the Menzies era could continue without him. In fact, the Liberal Party stayed in power, largely following his policies until 1972; and when the electorate chose to replace it with the Labor Party under Gough Whitlam, it was as much out of a sense of optimism for a new future as from a boiling discontent with the present. The late 1960s had seen vigorous dissent at Australia's

Vietnam policy, but the protests never reached the nationally divisive proportions found in the United States; in any event, the last combat troops were withdrawn in 1971. But the 1970s, a decade that began with aspirations higher than ever before, proved to be a time of disappointment and uncertainty.

The Whitlam government began its term with a series of enthusiastic reforms that were mostly welcomed — and, in many cases, long overdue. A national health service was organized, pensions and benefits were increased to the levels prevailing in most advanced countries, and significant amounts of money were at last spent upon the Aboriginal community. Whitlam also re-

laxed restriction on Asian immigration, as much to appease Australia's trading partners as to provide the country with immigrants. But the government soon began to run into economic difficulties, and it was not helped by the world oil crisis of 1973. The government's popularity gradually decreased.

The way the Whitlam government was ousted was unique in the history of the Australian constitution. The Senate — which Labor did not control — took the unprecedented step of blocking a money bill, effectively paralyzing government; and the governor general, the queen's representative in Australia, took the equally unprecedented — to many Australians, shocking —

step of dismissing Prime Minister Whitlam. He then installed Whitlam's Liberal opponent, Malcolm Fraser, at the head of a caretaker government and called an immediate election. Fraser won easily, but resentment at the action of the governor general was deep, and for the first time, a significant number of voices could be heard calling for a republican constitution.

Fraser's government was soon almost as unpopular as its predecessor. The continued world recession was partly at fault, and Fraser's determination to reduce government expenditures and lessen the role of government won him many electoral enemies.

Australians were also becoming aware of a new threat from Southeast Asia — no longer military but economic. In 1970, Australia saw itself as the region's center of high technology; by 1980, the colossal dynamism of Singapore, Taiwan and South Korea — not to mention the continuing development of Japan — was a challenge to Australia's supremacy and left it with a growth rate well below that of its competitors. The neighbors were catching up.

As a result, Australians entered the 1980s much less sure of themselves than they had ever been before. Perhaps that was good: In the past, their self-assurance had often led to complacency and worse. When the Labor Party, under its new leader Robert Hawke, took power from Fraser in a surprise election victory in 1983, it was not a desire for socialism that inspired the electorate, but hope — the same hope for renewal that had elected Whitlam 11 years before. And if Australians no longer thought themselves so favored by fortune as they had a few years before, they still had a good deal to hope about. □

THE POLITICAL POWER STRUCTURE

GOVERNOR GENERAL

FEDERAL PARLIAMENT

PRIME MINISTER

CABINET

SENATE

HOUSE OF REPRESENTATIVES

STATE PARLIAMENTS

ELECTORATE

DIRECTLY ELECTED INDIRECTLY ELECTED

As the representative of the British sovereign, the governor general serves as Australia's head of state. Although he retains certain prerogatives, his role is largely ceremonial, and the real focus of power is the Cabinet, headed by the prime minister.

The prime minister is also the leader of the majority party in the House of Representatives, the lower chamber of the Federal Parliament and the main political battleground. The Senate, or upper house, acts as a legislative watchdog, with the right to amend or

veto any bill passed by the lower house. The 76 senators are elected every six years; the representatives, from 148 constituencies, serve three-year terms.

There are also elections for each of the six state parliaments. The state parliaments have considerable autonomy and possess virtually the same law-making powers for the territory under their jurisdiction as the Federal Parliament does for the nation. In the event of a conflict between state and federal laws, however, it is the federal laws that take precedence.

With candles to light their way underground, miners pose at the head of a shaft.

Smoke rises from the South Blocks Mine at the southern end of the lode.

EARLY DAYS AT BROKEN HILL

In 1883, tin was discovered at Broken Hill, a low, jagged ridge 120 miles from the nearest settlement in the New South Wales outback. The site subsequently also proved rich in silver, lead and zinc, but the settlers who flocked there faced harsh privations in the unforgiving semidesert; drought, dust storms, scurvy, typhoid, lead poisoning from the mines and fatal accidents underground made their lives precarious and punishing.

Over the years, the community struggled toward stability. By 1910, when the first generation of children were young adults, steam trolleys ran in the main street and the more affluent families gave formal names to their corrugated-iron dwellings. Sports and outings afforded some relief from the toil and hardship of life.

A newspaper, the *Barrier Miner*, reported the community's activities, from family picnics to the works' sometimes abrasive labor relations. The journal's photographer was Joseph Wooler, a mill hand's son from Yorkshire. His photographs, some of which are reproduced here, give an eloquent picture of the rigors and rewards of life in an early Australian mining town.

A wedding group gathers outside the bride's home.

During a 1909 strike, workers converge on the company office.

Strollers pause in Argent Street, the town's main thoroughfare.

A corrugated-iron veranda shelters a mother and daughter.

Spectators fill the town stadium for a soccer match.

A family picnics under gum trees near a creek outside the town.

A couple takes a ride on one of the town's transport camels.

At Fremantle in Western Australia, jostling sheep stream on board a converted oil tanker for shipment to the Arabian Gulf, where they will be slaughtered according to Muslim ritual. Since 1970, Australia has become a major supplier of meat for the Middle Eastern market.

THE CURRENTS OF PROSPERITY

Australia is a land with a visibly high standard of living. Swimming pools glisten like sapphires in 1 out of 10 suburban gardens; yachts skim across the harbors and bays; roads are crammed with cars, of which there are at least five for every 10 people, a rate of ownership second only to the United States. The seemingly endless stretch of suburban houses may be monotonous to the beholder, but two thirds of the houses — a higher proportion than in most European countries — are owner-occupied. And visiting one of those homes would confirm the impression that what ordinary Australians want, they can usually get. Color television? Eight out of 10 homes had sets within 18 months of their being put on the market in 1974. Refrigerators? Only 3 percent of the households in Australia are without one. And the purchase of these and other consumer goods has not exhausted the average family's disposable income; Australia has more savings accounts than people.

Nor do Australians have to work especially hard for their high standard of living. Effective trade unions, to which more than half the work force belongs, have helped to give Australian workers some of the best conditions in the world. Having secured a 40-hour week for most workers by the early 1950s, unions mounted a campaign for a 35-hour week in 1980 and have already achieved it in some industries. They have also won annual vacation time of four — in many cases, five — weeks, plus a generous sprinkling of official holidays. Besides Christmas and Easter, Australians also have days off for agricultural shows, the birthday of the Queen and, in the case of Melburnians, for the Melbourne Cup, the nation's premier horse-racing event.

To help them enjoy their holidays, Australians get a bonus of 17.5 percent of their wages for the vacation period. Four out of 5 people can afford to spend the time traveling away from home. In addition to the popular activities of camping out and vacationing in RVs, new diversions that cater mainly to the affluent middle class have been developed. An explosion of interest in skiing means that the winter resorts of the Australian Alps in the southeast are filled to capacity. On any weekend, the wineries of Victoria's Murray Valley, South Australia's Barossa Valley, Western Australia's Swan Valley and the Hunter Valley, north of Sydney, are bustling with visitors sampling the quality vintages. New summer resorts are mushrooming along the coasts of New South Wales and Queensland, as an increasing number of people buy holiday and retirement homes.

The first-time visitor to the continent might agree that Australia is indeed what Donald Horne called it in the title of his best-selling book *The Lucky Country* — a country where "Australians can live the life of the Mediterranean or the South Seas." However, another commentator, Craig McGregor, has detected a darker undertone to this hedonism: "It is almost as if Australians are out for a good time because they suspect it won't last."

His suspicions may be well founded, for in the early 1980s, it seemed that Australia's spending spree might have temporarily come to an end. In 1982, the country had slipped to 15th position in the Organization for Economic Cooperation and Development's rating of comparative living standards, having placed fifth in 1955. In the same year, 1 out of 10 workers—mostly young people—were unemployed, and the annual rate of inflation stood at more than 10 percent. Ominously, the nation's economic growth was being exceeded by the fast-emerging economies of the Pacific basin — not only by Japan, whose own stunning postwar growth had stimulated much of Australia's development, but also by the newly industrialized countries, such as South Korea, Thailand and Malaysia. Retail sales and building starts were static. Against other currencies, the Australian dollar was sliding. Factory production was at a four-year low. And to top it off, serious drought resulted in the poorest harvest for a decade, with some grain-producing regions experiencing their worst wheat yields since 1944.

For those Australians not too busy enjoying the pubs, clubs, barbecues and beaches, it seemed that the luck many had come to see as their national birthright was deserting them. Robert Hawke, the Labor prime minister who took office in March 1983, thought so too. "There used to be some validity in the description of Australia as the lucky country," he told the nation. "But in the seventies the succession of fortuitous circumstances ceased. The coun-

try should be brought to realize that it is no longer lucky. It has to do its own thinking and planning."

The fortuitous circumstances to which Hawke was referring stemmed from the fact that Australia is blessed with almost-unlimited resources of food, minerals and energy, and in the past, a minimum of effort and entrepreneurial skill had converted them into the export and income that enabled Australia to buy the good life. Before World War II, Australia was a giant farm, supporting itself by means of exports of wool and food to the industrialized nations of the West. At the time, people said that the nation lived off the sheep's back. But as luck would have it, the country was also a giant quarry, and around 1960, mineral resources began to challenge agriculture in importance. All the nation had to do to get rich, it

seemed, was to sell off chunks of the continent to the manufacturing nations, where pieces of Australia would miraculously be transformed into the consumer goods that fill Australian homes. In referring to the need for Australia to do "its own thinking and planning," Hawke was drawing attention to the risks inherent in an economy overreliant on primary products, many of them vulnerable to cyclical depressions in world trade.

Old habits are hard to break, however, especially when they have led to success in the past. At the turn of the century, the export earnings generated by the sale of wool, wheat, meat and other agricultural products helped to give the country one of the highest per capita incomes in the world; and by the beginning of World War II, the health of the economy was still based on an agricultural trade heavily dependent on overseas markets, especially Britain. In 1932, the Imperial Economic Conference in Ottawa led to an agreement that guaranteed an export market for Australian agricultural products in Britain, in return for preferential tariff treatment for British manufactured goods. The result was that almost half of Australia's imports in 1937 and 1938 came from the mother country, as did 55 percent of its export earnings. Australia itself manufactured a small but growing proportion of its goods; the number of people employed in manufacturing increased more than 50 percent between the wars.

World War II disrupted this pattern completely. Almost totally cut off from its major European customers and suppliers, Australia was forced to develop its domestic industry, including the manufacture of war-related products, such as ships, munitions, aircraft and chemicals. The severing of the traditional trading ties also encouraged Australia to direct trade away from Europe — a trend that was to gather momentum after 1945 in the burgeoning of commercial links with the United States and the countries of the Pacific basin.

At the end of the war, Australia was committed to a program of full employment. The postwar Labor government had greater centralized power — at the expense of the six states — than any previous federal administration, and it drew up plans for major national development projects, designed partly to meet the possibility of unemployment in an anticipated postwar depression and partly to show off the dynamism of the Australian economy.

The greatest single public-works effort was the Snowy River project. Established in 1949, the plan was to divert

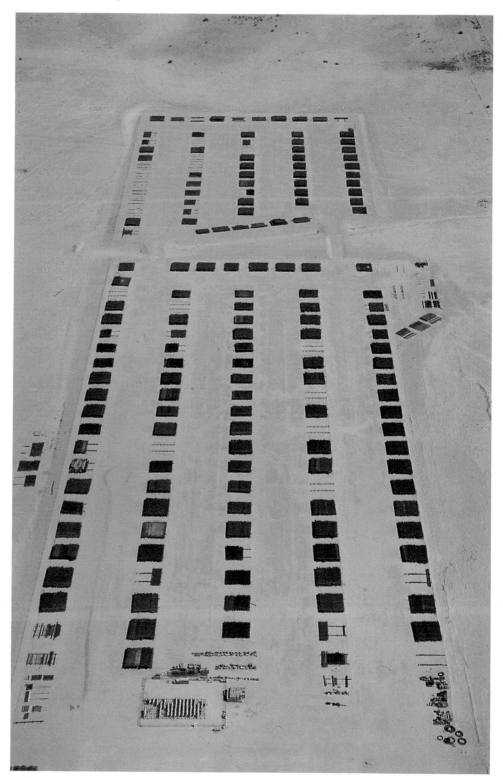

AN UNEXPECTED GIFT OF THE SEA

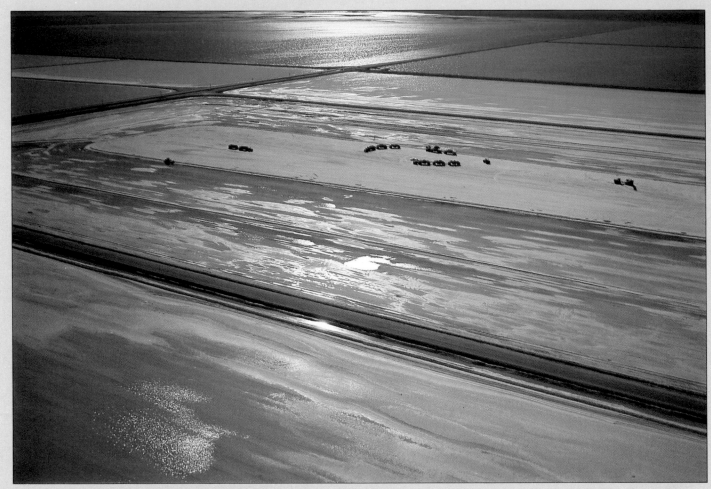

At the Dampier salt project in Western Australia, harvesters and road trains among the crystallizing ponds dot the stark white of a salt field.

Sun and sea — abundant in Australia — combine to create the salt-making process. Over much of the country, the evaporation rate far exceeds rainfall. Where these conditions occur near tidal flats, salt may be extracted from sea water on a large scale and at a low cost. Australia produces 6.7 million tons of salt a year, more than half of it at Western Australia's four salt fields — from Port Hedland in the far north to Shark Bay, about 400 miles up the coast from Perth.

It takes about 60 tons of sea water — and a lot of time — to make one ton of salt. The brine flows through a series of evaporation ponds; it takes about 18 months for the concentration of salt to rise from 2.5 percent to 20 percent. When the solids are ready to separate out, the brine is pumped into crystallizing ponds; six months later, a bed of white crystals forms. Then mechanical harvesters move in to scoop the salt onto road trains at a rate of 1,000 tons an hour. Washed clean of impurities and unwanted minerals, the salt is drained for three months, then taken to Dampier for export.

Clean washed salt pours from a conveyor onto a glittering stockpile to drain dry.

A road train is loaded with salt for export. Almost all of Western Australia's salt goes to Japan.

westward and under a wild region of the Australian Alps part of the flow of the Snowy River, which hitherto had flooded tempestuously to the Victorian coast. Tunnels blasted through the mountains carried the Snowy's waters into the Murrumbidgee and Murray rivers, increasing fivefold the amount of water available for irrigation downstream, in the fruit-growing and grazing districts of New South Wales and Victoria. And since the elevation of the headwaters of the Snowy was about 2,300 feet higher than that of the Murray, the water dropping from one to the other was also used to generate electricity. Completed in 1974, the project now provides about 20 percent of Australia's electric power, as well as irrigation for about 1,000 square miles of agricultural land.

Although the Snowy and other projects were of incalculable value in fostering a national sense of achievement, they would have been white elephants if growth in the manufacturing industry had not been sustained — which meant attracting overseas investment. Before the war, more than three quarters of Australia's national borrowing had been undertaken by federal and state governments and public authorities, with most of the money coming from London. But both the postwar Labor government and its successor, the long-running Liberal-Country administration under the leadership of Sir Robert Menzies, recognized the need for private capital from overseas. They had little difficulty locating funds. By the mid-1950s, about 70 percent of the foreign capital came from private international investors, attracted by the nation's untapped riches, by its political stability and by the probusiness attitude of the Menzies government.

A truck leaves the Jabiluka uranium mine in the Northern Territory, passing a geiger counter that checks its radiation level. Australia has about one fifth of the world's easily recoverable uranium reserves; most is sold under strict controls for generating electricity by nuclear reactors.

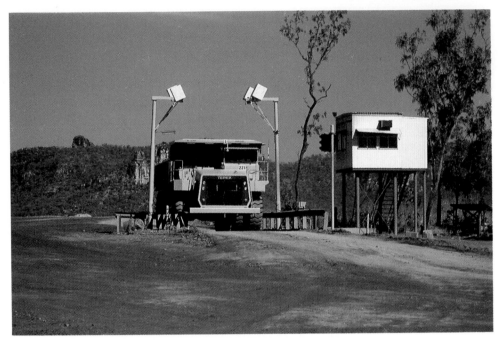

The major source of this private-sector investment was the United States. Canberra's closer political and defense links with Washington were mirrored by the growing importance of American business in Australia — at the expense of British investment. American capital, for example, was responsible for the entire development and promotion of the Holden automobile, which was made in Sydney and marketed as Australia's own. Although the British Motor Corporation also began automotive production in Australia in the 1950s, the battle for the driver's seat was won decisively in the end by American interests. General Motors (the manufacturers of the Holden) and Ford virtually monopolized the booming market for large, six-cylinder family sedans and station wagons.

Growth in manufacturing was also accelerated by the imposition of import restrictions in 1952 — a step taken to protect the nation's foreign exchange rates. The metal trades, also cushioned by high customs duties on goods of foreign origin, grew so fast that they were employing almost 50 percent of the manufacturing work force by the 1960s. The cities were alive with the throb of heavy industry. New enterprises began. Aluminum was transmuted in electric furnaces; tin-plate and steel mills began to roll. Oil, chemicals and shipbuilding were on a rising curve, and the scent of new opportunities for Australia was in the air.

None of this growth could have been achieved if there had not been more workers than ever before to keep the wheels of production turning. At the end of the war, the population of Australia stood at little more than seven million, and it was not highly qualified in terms of education. In 1938, only 25 percent of the teenagers had attended secondary school; as a result, the country lacked the skills necessary for the new industries. "Populate or perish" became a national slogan. It reflected both the need to increase the labor force and a sense of insecurity at a time when the nationalist and communist movements in Southeast Asia were signaling the end of direct European influence in the area. Because the British Isles — the traditional source of immigration — failed to satisfy the need, the Labor government was obliged to look elsewhere, particularly to displaced persons from the Baltic states and central Europe. Immigrants came flooding in from Greece, Yugoslavia, Holland, Italy, West Germany, the United States and Scandinavia. Almost three quarters of the one million increase in the work force between 1941 and 1961 were "migrants," as Australians call immigrants who have come to stay. Greece alone supplied so many that Melbourne, the new home city for most, soon housed the third-largest Greek community in the world.

Some of the migrants took rural jobs — like the Spanish farmworkers who became Queensland sugar-cane cutters, or the Italian tenant farmers who set up market gardens on the outskirts of the cities. But most went into manufacturing, working beside the native Australians and British migrants in the expanding factories and workshops. Some of these migrants became captains of postwar Australian industry: Sir Peter Abeles, a Hungarian refugee, who started work as a truckdriver and eventually became chairman of the international travel conglomerate TNT; Sir Tristan Antico, an Italian, who founded Pioneer Concrete Services; Sir Arvi Parbo, the Estonian-born chairman of Western Mining Corporation, who saw his firm's activities help spark the mining boom of the late 1960s.

The British immigrants continued to dominate the influx, however, partly as a result of travel subsidies designed to boost their numbers. In return for a commitment to work in Australia for a specified period of time, they were reimbursed for the cost of their trip, minus £10 — a scheme that earned them the sobriquet "ten-pound poms."

One of the most successful of the new Australians, and certainly the most flamboyant, has been Alan Bond, who arrived in Perth in 1950 with his family. Bond's father, who was in poor health, had decided to leave his native London for a warmer climate. At the age of 15, two years after he arrived in Australia, Bond left school and became an apprentice signwriter for a minimal weekly wage; by the time he was 19, however, he had formed a painting, decorating and repair company, taking on "jobs no one else would do," he recalls.

House painting was only a beginning, and he soon moved into one of the traditional Australian business activities — real estate speculation. For his first big deal, he borrowed a substantial amount of money to buy land on the outskirts of Perth: "I built asphalt roads there and subdivided the land and sold it cheaply. After four months I had paid back the bank, and the rest was profit." Bond was off and running, buying land and then subdividing it into 10,000-square-foot residential blocks in a succession of shrewd, if often risky, deals. In the mid-1960s, one of his boldest gambles was to develop a tract of sand dunes 36 miles north of Perth as a yachting center and holiday resort called Yanchep Sun City.

Surrounded by ranks of kangaroo-skin koala bears, an employee in a Perth toy factory knots a bow to add the final touch to the product. Two million or more kangaroos are culled each year: The skin is used for such consumer goods as handbags, and the meat is sold to the pet-food industry.

Bond's purpose was not only to make money but to create a base from which he could mount a challenge for the most prestigious trophy in yachting, the America's Cup, which had been held by the New York Yacht Club for more than a century.

Bond's first challenge failed, and there was worse to come. The property boom that had fueled his ambition collapsed in 1974, and it seemed that his business career would be set back to Square 1. But he survived and even managed to sell Sun City to Japanese buyers in order to fund his next venture: investment in Australia's booming energy developments.

Once again, he was in the right place at the right time. In 1978 he bought a stake in the Cooper Basin, a semi-desert region on the South Australia-Queensland border that was already supplying natural gas by pipeline to

Adelaide and Sydney. In the year of his acquisition, however, substantial oil reserves were also discovered. The find boosted Bond's capital dramatically. It allowed Bond to finance the acquisition of Western Australia's only brewery, Swan, and it also procured him an interest in a diamond mine in the northwest corner of the state.

With his second fortune, Bond renewed his quest for the elusive America's Cup. Although another attempt in 1980 had ended in failure, on September 26, 1983, his larger-than-life story became part of Australian sports mythology. Tied 3-3 with its rival after six races, his yacht *Australia II* surged ahead of the American boat *Liberty* in the decisive seventh race to take the most jealously guarded trophy in sports history. A quest that had cost Bond a sizable fortune over a period of 10 years had finally ended in triumph, and the celebrations that kept millions of Australians up all night were for him a personal fulfillment.

When Alan Bond arrived in Australia, agriculture was still providing almost 90 percent of the export earnings. More than half that total came from wool, with wheat, dairy products, meat and sugar making up the balance. Australia, it was estimated, owned roughly one sixth of the global sheep flock, from which it produced about one quarter of the world's wool.

Not surprisingly, then, the mainstay of country life was, as it continues to be, sheep ranching, and its most respected citizens are the graziers — landowners with large holdings dating back in many cases to the days of the original "squattocracy." By their prosperity and the scope of their social life — incorporating balls, polo, European travel and

THE SUBTERRANEAN LIFE OF THE OPAL MINERS

A tourist bus stands among the spoil heaps that lie by each mineshaft in the opal fields. Visitors may sift through the heaps for stray stones.

A sign warns of the danger of abandoned mineshafts in the town.

Miners in a rocky gallery work with pick and shovel.

Opals were discovered in 1915 at Coober Pedy, an isolated spot in the center of South Australia, thousands of miles from the nearest town. The town now houses more than 4,000 inhabitants and is still the main opal-producing center in Australia — or anywhere else. Ninety percent of the world's opals come from Coober Pedy or from nearby Andamooka.

In spite of continuous mining since 1916, it is estimated that less than 2 percent of the existing opal stock has been brought to the surface. Mining operations are kept to a small scale by government regulations. The law permits each miner to stake only one claim and limits that claim to an area of 540 square feet. No more than four people may form a partnership. So large mining concerns have no place in the town, which remains a rough and ready community of individuals hoping to make a fortune by their own efforts.

To get a chance at wealth, the miners contend with a multitude of discomforts — the worst is extreme heat. Four months of the year, the average temperature is 97° F., rising to 104° F. or more for days. Dust from the mining often swirls into blinding storms that make taking off and landing at the rocky airstrip nerve-racking. The only water comes from a saline well, and the fresh water provided by a solar-desalination still is precious: Each resident is allowed 120 gallons a week.

To escape the crushing heat, many people at Coober Pedy have retreated underground, into caves dug out of the slope where the opals were first discovered. The gypsum in the rocks makes it possible to hollow out sizable chambers that will not collapse. Some homes are spacious and even luxurious; and if the occupants decide to add a room by carving out the rock, there is always the chance that they may find a few gems.

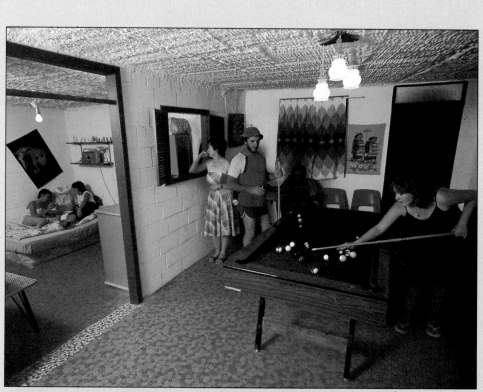
Miners relax with friends and family in one of the comfortable underground houses.

A priest celebrates a wedding in the grotto-like Anglican church opened in 1977.

3

In northern Queensland's moist tropical zone, where 95 percent of Australia's sugar-cane production is concentrated, flames race through the dry stalks of a plantation. The fields are burned off every winter to eliminate snakes, insects and debris that might hinder the cane cutters at harvesttime.

visits to the cities to see friends and attend agricultural shows — these native aristocrats distinguished themselves from the small-scale ranchers. Yet the ranchers also lived comfortably for the most part, in wide-verandaed homes, screened for protection against the ubiquitous bush flies.

A portrait of a typical small sheep rancher, then or now, would probably show a stocky figure with a frank and open countenance and a deeply tanned complexion. He would be dressed in elastic-sided boots, moleskin trousers, a checked shirt and would be wearing — with a self-consciousness that revealed unfamiliarity — a plain tie. But his country origins would be given away by a wide-brimmed hat, worn with pride perhaps bordering on ostentation. "The bigger the brim, the smaller the property," an ironic maxim warns.

The currency of such woolgrowers' lives is sheep fleece, and removing it has always been the main business of the station year. Freelance shearers, paid by the number of animals they clip, are hired for this work. Today, with the use of trail bikes for rounding up the sheep and aircraft for keeping track of them, the work has become increasingly mechanized and staffs have been shrinking; but in the postwar years, a number of resident hands were also needed to perform such tasks on the station as fencing, servicing the

84

windmills and pumps to ensure the water supply in artesian areas, protecting lambs from dingoes and other predators, and rounding up the sheep with the aid of kelpies and other sheep dogs.

The cattle stations — the other props of the pastoral economy — were even less labor-intensive. Most of them were unfenced and might consist of little more than a central homestead, around which the animals would roam at will within a radius of 10 miles or so; the limits were defined only by the need to return to the local watering place to relieve thirst.

Unsurprisingly, Australian members of the agriculture business in general, and the stock breeders in particular, were often accused of being unscientific and a trifle lackadaisical in their approach. Competition — in the case of wool, from synthetic fibers — and the threat to the farmers' traditional main market, as Britain negotiated for membership in the European Economic Community, forced a change of attitude. In an effort to remain competitive, Australian farmers used more machinery, adopted scientific breeding methods and increased the average size of their holdings — measures that reduced the rural labor force to about 1 in 20 by the 1960s. The ability to adapt to new conditions was well illustrated by the wool industry, which had accounted for as much as one third of Australian overseas sales in the prewar years but had been hit hard by the loss of markets during the war and by a severe drought in the mid-1940s. Thanks to better breeding techniques, pasture improvement and the introduction of the myxomatosis virus to control the plague of rabbits that had been ravaging the grazing land, wool output began to rise again at the beginning of the

1950s. The resurgence came in time for the farmers to cash in on a new demand for woolen garments, generated by the presence of thousands of American troops who were in Southeast Asia because of the Korean War. In five years, fleece prices increased tenfold.

By 1952, though, the pent-up spending power that was unleashed by these windfall earnings had produced the first of the postwar inflationary waves. When the boom burst, the credit squeeze that brought inflation down left woolgrowers with well-stocked pastures financed at high interest rates, but with dramatically reduced returns with which to pay off the loans. Faced with low prices and the contraction of the Yorkshire woolen mills that had provided the main market since the early days of settlement, many wool-

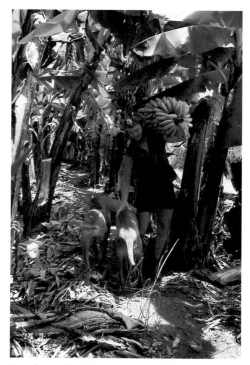

In a Queensland banana grove, dogs greet a worker bringing in a load of fruit. Pineapples, papayas and mangoes are also grown in Australia's tropical and subtropical regions, while the temperate areas produce apples, pears, plums and berries.

growers switched to wheat and cattle production; others sold out and joined the drift back to the cities.

But some graziers elected to ride out the recession, just as their fathers had decided to do in the Great Depression. Their optimism was justified. Although wool prices did not return to the levels of the early 1950s, the industry regained prosperity with new markets in the rapidly growing Japanese mills. In the 1970s, Japan's mills were joined by the fast-emerging woolen industries of South Korea and Taiwan. By the middle of the 1980s, in spite of desperate drought at the beginning of the decade, Australia was still the world's dominant wool exporter, producing almost a quarter of the global crop.

The pattern of finding new markets was repeated across a wide range of agricultural exports. Australian cattle growers, for example, climbed aboard the American fast-food bandwagon by producing the low-grade beef used for making hamburgers. By the 1970s, the United States was Australia's biggest customer for beef. And the drive for new markets knew no political barriers, as the wheat board proved: It was able to make significant grain sales to the People's Republic of China at a time when the Canberra government did not recognize the Communist administration in Peking.

By the 1980s, agriculture was contributing 6 to 7 percent of Australia's output, and though this figure was well below the 20 percent of 1900, one third of the export earnings were made by rural products. Wool was being challenged by wheat as the chief farm export. The nation was still the second-largest sugar exporter in the noncommunist world, with overseas sales in excess of A$700 million in 1982. And the

3

At Port Lincoln in South Australia, a worker swings a load of tuna onto a trailer that will take the catch to a processing plant for canning. Tuna accounts for more than one quarter of Australia's total fish yield.

beef market, buoyed by its new American customers, remained steady, with sales of more than A$1 billion in 1982.

And yet the postwar achievements of Australia's farmers have been eclipsed in the popular imagination by the success of the mining industry, which caused one of the wildest stock-market stampedes of this century. Almost every generation in Australia since the mid-19th century has caught the gambling fever produced by a major mineral discovery, but no one was prepared for the boom of the 1960s. Australia entered the decade as a country that banned iron-ore exports, had virtually no nickel production and had to import all but a trickle of its oil. Yet 10 years later, it was one of the world's leading iron-ore and nickel exporters and had lifted its crude-oil output from 5,000 to 65 million barrels a year. In the '60s, bauxite production increased twelvefold, manganese production multiplied 13 times, tin output quadrupled, black coal doubled, and copper and lead output improved by 50 percent.

Discoveries were made in all parts of Australia. On the island of Groote Eylandt in the Gulf of Carpentaria, massive deposits of manganese were found in 1966. In the same year, Australia's largest company, Broken Hill Proprietary (BHP), in partnership with the world's biggest petroleum company, Esso (later named Exxon), struck oil and gas in the Bass Strait. The field, between the Victoria coast and Tasmania, was to become the mainstay of the nation's supplies. The '60s also saw the development of the Weipa bauxite re-

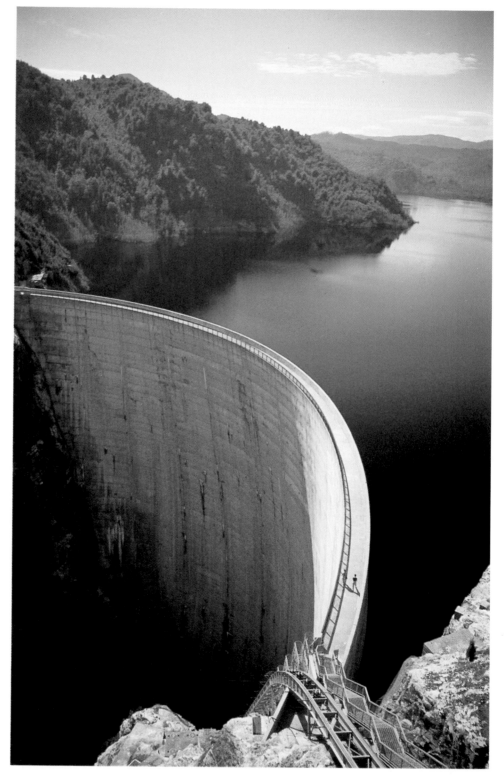

serves in the York Peninsula, which had been unearthed a few years before, and the opening of the huge Blackwater coal mine in central Queensland.

Perhaps the most spectacular discovery of the decade was made in the Pilbara region of Western Australia, where in 1938, the federal government had stopped the development of iron-ore reserves for strategic reasons. The ban remained in effect for 15 years after the war, because of a gloomy warning made by the official government geologist in 1938 "that if known supplies of high-grade ore are not conserved, Australia will become an importer rather than a producer of ore."

One man who knew that this view was wrong was Lang Hancock, a stock breeder in the Pilbara. In November 1952, he and his wife had been flying across the Hamersley Range when a storm forced their plane below cloud level. Hancock noticed a metallic sheen in the 200-foot-high cliffs of the gorge in which he was flying. It indicated that they might be rich in iron, and when he returned later to verify this, he found that he was not mistaken. Hancock kept the secret to himself, but when the ban was lifted in 1960, he took executives of the British mining house Rio Tinto Zinc to the area, where geologists traced bands running for hundreds of miles across the ranges. Asked to estimate the amount of reserves in the region, an American steel executive replied that it was like trying to "calculate how much air there was"; workers boasted that one mountain was so rich in iron ore that it rusted in the rain.

The discoveries could not have been better timed, since world iron and steel production expanded dramatically in the 1960s. Japan, in particular, developed an insatiable demand for ore to

A WORLD CENTER OF PEARLING

The ketch-rigged pearling luggers that operate out of Broome, more than 1,200 miles north of Perth in Western Australia, have not changed much since they were first used in the 1880s, but the pearling industry — one of Australia's oldest — has been through many vicissitudes. Even before the luggers arrived, divers were collecting high-quality pearl shells from the tropical waters offshore. By 1910, Broome was the world's biggest pearling center, with up to 400 craft crewed by Japanese, Malays, Filipinos, Chinese and others. They faced great hardships, from cyclones to the decompression sickness known as the bends, to bring home the shell that supplied the world's demand for mother-of-pearl.

Broome's prosperity declined in subsequent decades, partly as a result of two world wars, partly because plastics began to erode the market for mother-of-pearl. But after World War II, new techniques for culturing pearls revived the fortunes of the community. By the early 1980s, there were five thriving pearl-culture farms in the town's vicinity, and pearls and pearl shells were a multimillion dollar industry.

The luggers' pearling trips to the oyster beds four miles off the coast are normally limited by tidal conditions to 10 days' duration. The pearler's year is divided into three seasons. Between April and August, young shell is separated from the large pearl shells and kept alive aboard ship in tanks of circulating sea water; on the farms it is seeded to produce cultured pearls. From September to December, only large shells are collected; they provide mother-of-pearl for the manufacture of knife handles, buttons, furniture inlays and similar articles. The wet season — December to March — means a rest for the crews, and the luggers are laid up on the beach.

Two pearling luggers sail out to the oyster beds. Each can bring back as many as 6,000 young oysters.

In a shed on land, a mountain of large shells is sorted and graded.

Oysters drying in the sun festoon the rigging of a lugger, while the crew sorts and packs the shells.

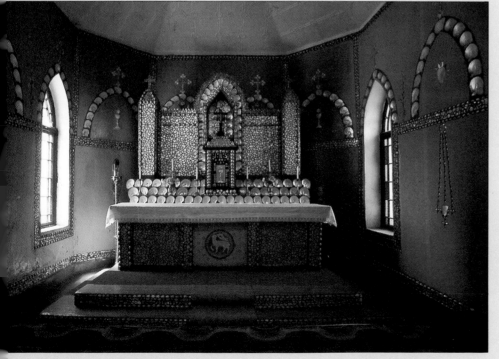
The Catholic church at Beagle Bay, 80 miles north of Broome, shimmers with pearl shell.

feed its steel industry, which quadrupled output between 1960 and 1970. Australia had to call on foreign capital to develop the Pilbara, and companies such as Kaiser, AMAX and Mitsui joined the Australian companies CSR and BHP to invest hundreds of millions of dollars. The money was spent on building ports such as Dampier and Port Hedland, establishing new towns in the Western Australia outback and laying railroad tracks for thousands of miles across the desert.

On April 4, 1966, as the development of the Pilbara region was getting under way, attention was diverted by the announcement of another discovery 600 miles to the south, near the historic mining town of Kalgoorlie, the scene of the gold rushes of the 1890s. This time the mineral involved was nickel, which 17th-century metallurgists called "devil's copper" because of its resemblance to that valuable metal. It lighted the fuse for the biggest Australian stock-market explosion of the century.

The timing of the strike was crucial. The American aerospace and defense industries involved in the Vietnam War and the space race had a boundless appetite for nickel at a time when the world's major producer, Canada, was having supply problems. To capitalize on this demand, Western Mining Corporation, which had made the discovery, developed the nickel mine with unprecedented speed; within a year of the announcement of the strike, ore was being produced, and by August 1967, the first shipments of nickel concentrate had been dispatched. But while Western Mining made the discovery, the company that rocked the international investment world in the nickel boom was Poseidon — a symbol of the get-rich-quick fever gripping Austra-

3

lia. In 1969, Poseidon shares stood at 80 cents; in April 1970, after its miners had made a nickel discovery at Windara in Western Australia, its shares had soared to A$286. And yet all the company possessed at the time was a row of drill holes, a line of trenches and some rough mining camps in the bush.

Nickel hysteria swept Australia; there were tips that Poseidon would go to A$500 a share. Rumors of fresh strikes sent waves of prospectors to stake mining claims in the most unlikely areas. New companies having only the most tenuous connections with mineral exploration were floated almost daily on the stock exchange. Many joined the boom by changing their names: Glacarium, which owned an ice rink in Sydney, became Nickel Development; Project Development, which built houses and sold meat, became Project Mining. Ordinary people who had never bought a share in their lives began wagering on a dizzy assortment of facts, half-truths and bare-faced lies. Dubious practice was rife. After its chairman told a reporter that his nickel prospects could be bigger than Poseidon's, shares in one mining company rose from A$3 to A$96 in three days. The stock prices subsequently collapsed, and a report found that the prospect consisted of "a few panned samples and a hazy identification of some excavated rock."

It was not just Australia that was infected by the nickel bug. The rest of the world joined in, quadrupling overseas investment on the Australian stock market between 1966 and 1971. These funds — known as "hot money," because of their short-term duration in the country — in combination with hundreds of millions directly invested in long-term projects, pushed foreign capital to torrential levels, fueling fears that Australia had sacrificed its economic independence for a fast buck.

With newspapers filled with stories of traders making thousands of dollars a day, most Australians must have felt they were on the verge of the greatest era of prosperity in their history. Few heeded what the bush poet Banjo Paterson had written at the turn of the century: "I saw bank booms, land booms, silver booms, Northern Territory booms, and they all had one thing in common — they always burst."

And so it happened with the minerals boom. With so much of the Australian mining industry mortgaged to the needs of the Western industrialized nations, it took only a fall in demand to prick the bubble. That came in 1971, when the Nixon administration, faced with soaring trade deficits, imposed a surcharge on imports. Japan, America's major trading partner, was forced to cut back on exports; its demand for raw materials, of which Australia was a major supplier, was thereby reduced. In 1972, Japanese steel mills were unable to honor contracts to take 100 million tons of Australian iron ore. In 1974, when the U.S. dollar crisis had eased and economic recovery seemed to be under way, the oil crisis intervened, again cutting manufacturing in the industrialized nations and reducing their imports of raw materials.

For Australia, the resultant problems were compounded by factors that weakened the nation's ability to compete in world markets. At the start of the 1970s, when unemployment stood at 2 percent, the unions had the upper hand and were quick to use it. The number of strikes rose sharply as unions confronted labor-starved employers with wage demands. In 1971, earnings rose by 13 percent, compared

In a warehouse at Kwinana, a port 20 miles south of Perth, a team of government inspectors takes samples of a mountainous store of wheat awaiting export, to ensure that it is free of insects. Australia is the world's third-largest exporter of wheat, surpassed only by the United States and Canada.

with an annual average for the previous decade of 5 percent. Inevitably, wage increases were reflected in higher prices, and inflation, which had averaged 2.5 percent in the 1960s, rose to 6 percent in 1971 and 8 percent in 1972.

The difficulties of limiting wage settlements to a level acceptable for the economy as a whole were exacerbated by the system of labor relations. The work force is highly unionized but split among more than 300 unions, operating within a legally established system of arbitration commissions at federal and state levels. Although the Australian Council of Trade Unions tries to coordinate its members, it has little power. Membership in a union allows an Australian to gain not only a national wage increase (given to all workers, unionized or not) and an industry-wide award that ensures parity with other industries, but also an "over-award" wage hike negotiated with each employer.

With the unions exercising the considerable leverage they commanded, wages increased by 29 percent in 1974 and 15 percent in 1975, and prices rose 15 percent and 13 percent respectively in the same years. Business, struggling with accelerating costs and double-digit interest rates, reduced investment by 5 percent, plunging the country further into recession. The economy, which had been growing by 7 percent per year at the start of the decade, stagnated. The gloom in industry was summed up by a bumper sticker: "Will the last businessman to leave Australia please turn out the lights."

After more than a decade of virtually full employment, the number of people out of work more than doubled in 1974. Job losses were particularly severe in the textile, footwear and clothing industries, which had been hit hard by tariff cuts introduced by the 1972 Labor government. Layoffs were also heavy in the automotive industry, with reductions at Ford, Chrysler and General Motors Holden and the closing of British Leyland's plant in Sydney.

The unemployment continued to rise after the coming to power, in 1975, of Malcolm Fraser's Liberal-Country party, which had vowed to give priority to the fight against inflation. But despite tight budgetary and monetary policies, inflation did not return to single digits until 1978; and even then, price increases of 8 to 9 percent made Australian goods uncompetitive in the international marketplace. As so often in the past, when economic salvation came in 1979 and 1980, it came not so much from Australian economic policies as from events outside — this time, another oil crisis in the Middle East.

Australia was in a better position to weather the new oil crisis than most countries, thanks to the development of the Bass Strait fields, which ensured that at least 70 percent of the country's needs could be met from its own resources. In addition, a string of discoveries and developments in the 1970s had reconfirmed Australia's position as a major exporter of energy. The huge coal strip mines of central Queensland were expanding output; oil and gas finds in the Cooper Basin were substantial enough to justify the construction of a huge liquefied-petroleum-gas production plant; and the discovery of large deposits at Roxby Downs had quadrupled the nation's uranium reserves. Coal, which in the early 1970s accounted for less than 5 percent of Australia's overseas income, became the country's most important commodity, constituting 14 percent of export sales in 1983 and making Australia one of the top three exporters in the world.

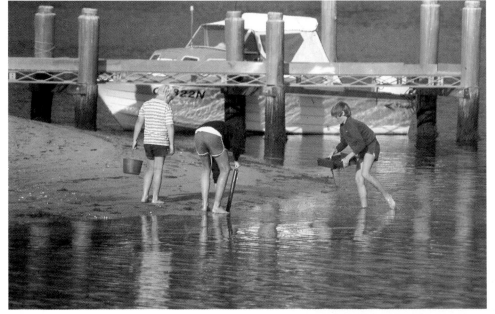

At the little town of Woy Woy, a retirement community and holiday resort 50 miles north of Sydney on the coast of New South Wales, children dig happily for crabs on the beach. Despite the economic fluctuations of recent years, most Australians can still enjoy a life rich in outdoor recreation.

As world energy prices continued to rise, many foreign countries decided to harness the continent's resources by locating energy-intensive industries, such as aluminum production, Down Under. At a time of world shortage of aluminum, Australia stood to reap huge benefits, but the rush to capitalize on the opportunity led to an unseemly squabble between states: Each state, irrespective of its energy capabilities, vied to offer the aluminum companies electricity at bargain-basement prices. Within two years, plans for the building or expansion of aluminum smelters were announced for Portland in Victoria, Gladstone in Queensland, and Tomago, Lochinvar and Kurri Kurri in New South Wales' Hunter Valley; and construction of a smelter at Wagerup in Western Australia was completed.

But by 1982, the world was in recession, reducing both the need for energy and resources. Once again the prophecy of Banjo Paterson had been fulfilled. When aluminum prices fell, the Portland smelter was shelved, the Lochinvar project was canceled, and the Kurri Kurri expansion was halted. In the same year, the Japanese announced that they were having second thoughts about taking liquefied petroleum gas from the Cooper Basin; they also cut coal imports from Australia and announced to Australian steel producers that they were substantially reducing their orders. The boom that had lifted the Australian economy in the early 1980s to a growth rate twice that of most major Western countries had fizzled almost before it had begun.

Unemployment, which had dipped slightly in 1980 and 1981, climbed to a postwar high, with 1 in 10 workers — about 600,000 people — out of work. Particularly depressing was the fact that 1 in 5 teenagers was jobless, and the average wait for a job after getting out of school had risen to 10 months. The jobless were cushioned to some extent by unemployment payments, but life on these was far from easy. In 1984, unemployment benefits for a single person aged 18 or older without dependents amounted to A$81 a week, and they were A$153 for a married man without dependents, compared with an average national income of A$300.

Of course, Australia was not the only country to feel the effects of recession in the 1980s, nor could all the blame for its economic misfortunes be laid on external factors. The boom of 1981 had recalled some of the worst aspects of the late 1960s, particularly in industrial relations. When workers in other industries saw the high wages being paid in the resource industry, the unions decided to press for increases beyond those recommended by the federal and state wage boards. The result was the worst outbreak of industrial disputes in 10 years, with employees in almost every sector resorting to strike action. During one especially bad period, Sydney had no electricity, trains, trash collection or telephones — prompting the exasperated newspaper headline, "Is anyone out there working?"

A frightening aspect of the unbridled wage demands was that they reduced Australia's competitive position against the fast-emerging economies of the Pacific basin. In the 10 years before 1983, Australia's average annual growth was 2.6 percent, compared with 3.7 percent in Japan and more than 7 percent in Taiwan, South Korea, Hong Kong, Singapore, Malaysia and Thailand. Forecasts suggest that the gap between Australia and its neighbors will close further, with Asian economies ex-

pected to grow by between 7 and 9 percent in the 1980s, while Australia maintains the pace it had in the 1970s. It was the need to place the economy on a more competitive basis that prompted Labor Prime Minister Robert Hawke — a former trade-union leader — to call a meeting of national business and union leaders after he took office in 1983.

After four days of debate, an accord was hammered out. The union leaders agreed to postpone indefinitely any new salary demands in exchange for price controls and a vast public-works program, aimed at creating jobs in Australia's sagging construction industry and other areas of the economy. The government also tried to make Australian industry more competitive internationally by opening the market to imported goods, hoping that Australian manufacturers, in order to survive, would start to produce technologically advanced products for the expanding economies of its neighbors.

In the wake of the conference, Australia stood at an economic crossroads. The choice was for the country to remain little more than a continent-wide quarry, letting other industrialized nations turn its vast natural resources into goods, or to use the skills of its work force and its businesses to become a major manufacturing power. Were it to succeed in the latter course, its economy could become one of the most dynamic in the region. Some years ago an American journalist described Australia as the Disneyland of the Pacific: "The size and scale of its resources development task made it Frontierland, Adventureland and Tomorrowland rolled into one. But there is a touch of Fantasyland about it too — will the development really take place, or is much of it wishful thinking?"   □

THE WEATHER'S UGLY MOOD

From time to time, the usually stable Australian climate turns cruelly capricious, causing damage on a grand scale. Normally, the continent is influenced by a mass of warm, moist air—centered over Indonesia to the northeast—which ensures that some rain will fall over most of the country. But every five years or so, a ridge of high pressure dominates the region, and that can mean no rain at all.

The phenomenon of recurring changes in the weather pattern, known to meteorologists as the Southern Oscillation and as yet unexplained, presages the coming of droughts that can turn the land to dust, kill off crops and livestock—and spell economic ruin for farmers. Another hazard of the dry spells are brush fires, which in bad years claim a harrowing share of forest and farmland.

The end of a drought, however, can bring its own dangers. The barometric pressure may decrease dramatically, causing torrential rains. Then enormous areas of topsoil, desiccated in the preceding months, are swept away by floods.

A swimmer runs for shelter as a dust storm sweeps across Port Phillip Bay toward Melbourne on February 8, 1983. Carried by winds from the drought-stricken outback, the storm raged over the city for 40 minutes, blinding motorists and blanketing the streets with 11,000 tons of topsoil.

94

Stirred by the spiraling updrafts of wind known as "willy willies," a haze of red dust hangs over the town of Pooncarie, in New South Wales.

Guarded by a lone fence, South Australian pastureland scorched by the sun stretches to a dusty horizon (*right*). When drought hits the land, it is usually the sheep and cattle ranchers who head the economic casualty list. As soil deteriorates and pastures are overgrazed, many ranchers sell their poorer-quality stock for rock-bottom prices and carry feed to the rest (*above*). But if the drought is prolonged, the feed may run out. Then the choice is moving the animals to expensive grazing areas or shooting them. Either way, years of work can be canceled out in a few months.

Brush fires sweep through tinder-dry forest in Victoria after a prolonged drought *(left)*. **Such conflagrations are a regular feature of life in the out-back, and each community has its own force of volunteer fire fighters, equipped with water pumps, walkie-talkies and fire extinguishers** *(above)*.

FLOOD: THE ORDEAL AFTER THE RAINS

A truck noses its way through the rain-flooded bush on Western Australia's Kimberley Plateau. The downpours that often follow a long spell of dry weather can inundate vast tracts of territory, disrupting transportation and communications and briefly turning the land into a huge lake.

With his dogs to help him, a grazier herds a flock of Merinos by motorcycle in the Riverina district of New South Wales. The dry grassland plains fringing the outback provide pasture for millions of sheep, which outnumber the human population of Australia almost 10 to 1.

THE MYSTIQUE OF THE OUTBACK

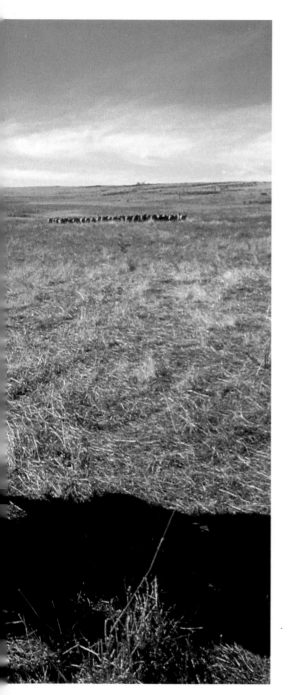

Behind the inhabited coastal fringes of Australia lie more than 3 million square miles of arid plains, marginal pastureland, deserts, scrub, salt lakes and worn-down mountain ranges that together make up the outback. The region has no formally defined boundaries — not, that is, unless you count the 6,000 miles of 6-foot-high fence built to keep dingoes (wild dogs) out of the Queensland and South Australia sheep country. The outback begins where the population density falls to a level that can be measured in square miles per person rather than in people per square mile. In Australia, that means about four fifths of the land area — almost the whole of the country west of the 3,000-mile Great Dividing Range, across which 19th-century explorers traveled in search of the vast inland sea that they were sure must lie at the heart of the continent.

But the explorers were geological ages too late. One hundred and fifty million years ago, during the Jurassic era, giant plesiosaurs with ranks of teeth in a 10-foot-long head hunted where now only salt pans shimmer in the sun; and 25,000 years ago, two-ton, plant-eating marsupials browsed on lush vegetation, which has now been replaced by sand dunes and stony gibber plains. Today, the bones of these creatures lie entombed under the salt crusts of lakes that may fill with water only once in a lifetime. There is rain in the Australian outback, but it is sporadic and can cause as much damage by flooding as the severe droughts that precede and follow it. Children who are born in one of the isolated settlements in the dry center of the continent may not see rain until they are more than five years old.

Not surprisingly, in view of the prevailing aridity, the principal color of the outback is brown. On its fringes, the land is khaki-toned and liberally sprinkled with the gray-green of water-conserving mulga and mallee shrubs. Scattered through its width are small townships — dusty settlements that often consist of a street of one-story buildings, many built out of corrugated iron. Between the towns there are only isolated homesteads, linked to one another and to civilization by lonely roads that are lined, perhaps, by a single telephone wire. Some of these homesteads are in the part of the outback that receives just enough rain to serve as pasture; others draw water from some of the thousands of artesian wells drilled into the huge underground reservoirs of the Great Artesian Basin, which underlies the outback's eastern section.

Much of the outback is genuine desert — or, to be more exact, many deserts, each one with its own individual character. North of Lake Eyre and straddling the state line of South Australia and Queensland is the Simpson Desert, a fiery gridiron of longitudinal dunes covering an area of 56,000 square miles. Here, in 1845, the explor-

4

In the heart of the outback, Alice Springs *(below)* is built over an artesian basin that provides water for trees and gardens. But rain is rare, and the lack of surface water is evident in the condition of the municipal golf course *(right)*, which is almost as dry and cracked as the surrounding desert.

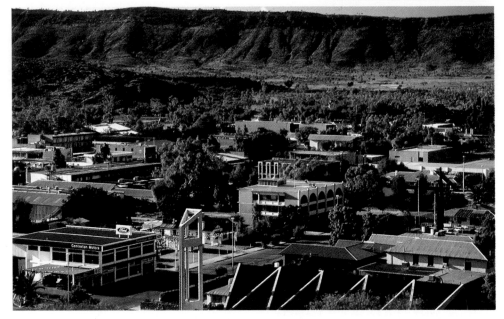

er Captain Charles Sturt and his party were marooned by drought for six months, surviving in an underground shelter as the temperature outside climbed to 128° F. With them they had a boat that they had dragged hundreds of miles to sail on the fabled inland sea. West of the Simpson, the red sand dunes give way to the thorny Great Victoria and Gibson deserts, the latter named after an explorer who died of thirst there in 1873. These deserts in turn give way to the Great Sandy Desert on Australia's northwest coast. In this region, the inhabitants of Marble Bar have to endure a mean December temperature of 93° F.; once, they experienced 160 consecutive days when, even in the shade, the temperature rose at least four degrees above that figure.

All these deserts surround the geographical heart of the continent. Here the color of the land deepens to tawny ocher, then to a sunburned red. This is Australia's Red Center, so called because of the iron oxide in the rocks, which turns them the color of rust. Worn flat by millennia of erosion, the Center survives immutable and immemorial, caught in a Sleeping Beauty trance from which only some great geological convulsion could awaken it. And at the midpoint of the Center itself is Ayers Rock — a smooth sandstone monolith rising 1,148 feet from a flat plain — one of the great natural wonders of the world.

Human works are few and far between in the outback, for such a hostile land cannot support a large population and probably never will. Western Australia, one quarter the size of Europe, has a population just over 1.25 million; most of the inhabitants live in Perth and the other coastal towns. The Northern Territory, covering 520,000 square

miles, is home to only a tenth that number, the majority in Darwin and Alice Springs. Outside the small townships, the outback population is scattered on sheep and cattle stations, some of which are as large as Belgium.

Roads are the main means of communication — long, unbroken stretches of dirt track with signs warning the driver that it is, say, 180 miles to the nearest available water. But the airplane too is an everyday lifeline, ferrying supplies to the dispersed oases of human habitation. QANTAS, Australia's international airline, started life in the outback as a one-plane service between remote bush settlements; the initials stand for "Queensland and Northern Territory Air Service."

Although the sprawling red outback, with its thin sprinkling of settlements, seems far removed from the bustling cities on the coastal fringe, the interior and its people remain an ever-present

force in Australian affairs. The outback lurks like some evil genie trapped in an insecurely corked bottle, and from time to time drought sets the genie free, reminding the coast dwellers how narrow their foothold in the country is. When the inland pastures have been seared by months of drought and the sheep and cattle have to be slaughtered and buried in mass graves, a cold wind can be felt in Australia's financial institutions, and the Sydney shopper who is faced with rising food prices receives a jolting reminder that the nation lives closer to the land than its population distribution would suggest. Since federation, most of the large swings in the fortunes of Australia's political parties have followed serious droughts.

Just how disastrous the absence of rain can be was brought home to Australians in 1983, the year that saw the climax of the prolonged drought they christened the Big Dry. All through

104

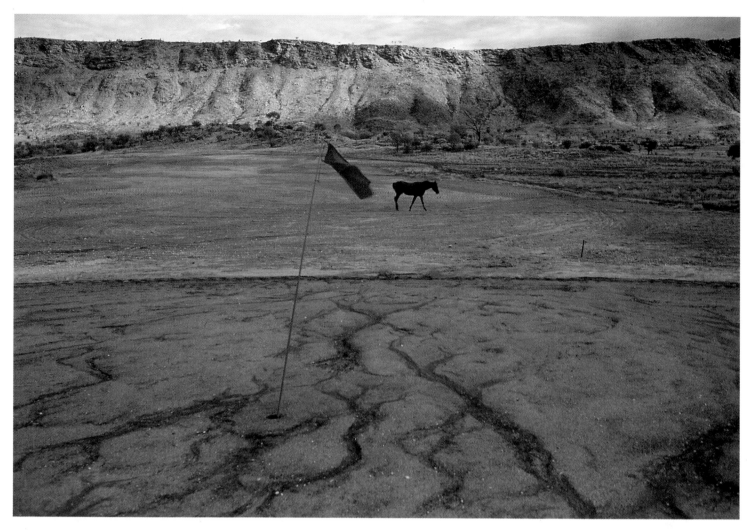

January, the country withered as strong winds whipped up the parched soil in the outback and carried it to the cities of the south and east, blinding motorists and clogging machinery. But worse was to come. On February 16 — Ash Wednesday — gale-force winds drove brush fires along 450 miles of coast from Adelaide to Melbourne. In some places, the fires caused a vacuum into which fireballs were sucked at speeds of more than 100 miles per hour. After two days, seven townships had been wiped out, some 2,000 homes had been destroyed, and more than 70 people had lost their lives.

For most of the nation's ranchers, the Big Dry lasted for two years. Faced with diminished reserves of fodder and overgrazed pastureland, many sheep ranchers had to cull their flocks and sell off all but their best ewes at rock-bottom prices. Some owners received only A$5 for animals that would normally have sold for A$20 to A$30 a head. They were the lucky ones: One New South Wales sheep rancher was forced to sell 180 of his ewes at 10 cents each. In parts of the Northern Territory, the drought — though less severe — went on for another six months, and when rains did come, they caused the worst flooding in 10 years.

Much of that torrential downpour was caused by a cyclone — another familiar weather hazard in the outback. The most disastrous of the great winds of recent years was the one that struck the city of Darwin on Christmas Day in 1974. Weather-satellite pictures had shown a large cloud mass in the Arafura Sea between Australia and New Guinea as early as December 21, and these clouds had taken on the ominous circular form typical of a developing typhoon. For the next three days the storm intensified, but its slow and steady course toward the southwest suggested that it would pass harmlessly north of the Australian coast, 60 miles or so out to sea.

But on the morning of December 24, Cyclone Tracy, as it was named, suddenly changed course to the southeast, on a direct line for the city. Weather officials who had been following the progress of the storm immediately notified the local federal authorities, who decreed that half-hourly cyclone warning messages should be transmitted on the local radio and television channels. But in the festive atmosphere of Christmas Eve, few people apparently paid much attention to the broadcasts. Attempts to convene a meeting of the local emergency committee failed, because most of the members proved to be inextricably enmeshed in the office-party circuit; amazingly, nobody even thought to forewarn the federal government officials in Canberra. The result was that the city was almost entirely unprepared when the cyclone struck in the early hours of Christmas Day.

The exact force of the wind is not known, because the Darwin airport anemometer broke when registering a speed of 165 miles per hour. The wind was so strong that it lifted roofs and cars and demolished whole stories of houses. When it abated some four hours later, 67 people were dead, and 90 percent of the buildings in the city had been devastated. Since Cyclone Tracy, Darwin has been rebuilt — for the third time, once after a cyclone in 1897, then following Japanese bombing in 1942. It has been estimated that a cyclone can be expected to pass within 60 miles of Darwin once every six years, so the permanence of the latest settlement cannot be taken for granted, despite all the precautionary measures to render the new structures windproof.

Natural disasters such as droughts and cyclones are tangible evidence of Australia's harsh nature, but for new-comers to Australia it is not just the outback's objective dangers that threaten. It is the land itself — its emptiness, its lack of definition, its unyielding primitivism, the bizarre character of its flora and fauna. A new generation of Australians, however, has come to appreciate the country's awesome beauty: the red monoliths of the Center; the rare water holes, cold and clear and deep; the primordial splendor of the vast, patterned landscapes laid out under a cerulean sky. For these people, the emptiness of the bush is its greatest asset, providing a refuge from the crowded and polluted cities and a source of spiritual renewal for those suffering from overexposure to the multiplying stimuli of modern life.

Tragically, the true heirs of the outback, the Aboriginals, have been dispossessed of their birthright, stripped of their culture and forced into a marginal existence on the fringes of white society, all in a relatively short time. When the first white settlers disembarked at Botany Bay in 1788, there were probably 300,000 Aboriginals in Australia and Tasmania, including the deserts of the outback. Between them, they spoke more than 500 different languages grouped into about 30 related language families, although one such family — the Pama-Nyungan — was used by more than 80 percent of the continent's population.

The Aboriginals were seminomadic hunter-gatherers in their traditional lifestyle, ranging over limited stretches of territory in their search for food and water. Various plants provided most of the foods in the desert tribes' diet, but meat was available for those who had learned to understand the bush's rhythms. Insects were commonly eat-

The sun's first rays light up verandas lining the main street of Coolgardie, in Western Australia's gold-mining district. Like many boom towns of the 1890s' gold rush, Coolgardie declined when the seams ran dry. Now with a resident population of about 700, tourism is its main resource.

en. The wichety grub — the larval stage of a moth — was considered a delicacy; honey ants and various species of bee supplied a source of sugar. Apart from lizards, larger animals were not everyday food items.

The men did most of the hunting. They speared kangaroos, emus, possums, snakes and the large lizards called goannas; trapped and caught other animals; speared or trapped fish. Coastal Aboriginals knew the places where whales stranded themselves. Most smaller food items — seeds, yams, roots, honey, fruits and berries — were collected by the women. The Aboriginals devoted much time and energy to the important task of locating water; they relied on memory and on good navigation skills to find the water holes and the soaks, or small marshy areas, whose locations they were taught from early childhood.

To catch large prey, Aboriginal men used a number of ingenious weapons; these included the woomera, or throwing stick, which could hurl a spear more than 300 feet, and the various kinds of boomerang, which were effective up to a distance of about 150 feet. The well-known returning boomerang was used mainly for games and for diverting prey into traps or ambushes. The women's essential tool was the coolomon — a curved dish, usually hollowed from a knot of wood, which was used for carrying water, digging for termites and other food, and pounding the seeds used to make bread. Apart from these items, the Aboriginals had few material possessions; those they did have were portable, so that the people could move quickly and take advantage of the seasonal changes. At night the Aboriginals slept out in the open air or in shelters made from the local vegetation. To keep warm, they lit fires by using friction sticks, or they simply curled up with each other or with the semidomesticated dogs — cousins of the dingo, which arrived on the continent with visiting seamen from the Asian mainland about 4,000 years ago.

Since the food resources of the outback are limited, the Aboriginals did most of their hunting and gathering in units of one or more nuclear families; but they owed their allegiance to tribes, formed by the splitting off of related groups after an increase in population and the consequent establishment of new territories. An individual's social obligations were dictated largely by observance of extremely sophisticated and complex kinship systems. Children were often betrothed at birth — and frequently, in the case of girls, to partners much older than themselves. Those who received a wife were generally obliged to make repayment at the time of the marriage or at some time in the future — usually in the form of an exchange of sisters. Although many men had only one wife at a time, the ramifications of the kinship system meant that men and women had available a number of potential partners, who provided them with an accepted channel for premarital or extramarital liaisons. Actual polygamy was sometimes practiced; some men had as many as 30 wives, the later ones often pressed on the husband by the first wives, who may have wished to reduce the burden of food gathering.

Despite the rigors of their harsh environment, the Aboriginals had a well-developed social life and a sense of esthetics. They held ritual gatherings that were attended only by men, but they also staged nonreligious ceremonies for both sexes, called corrobor-

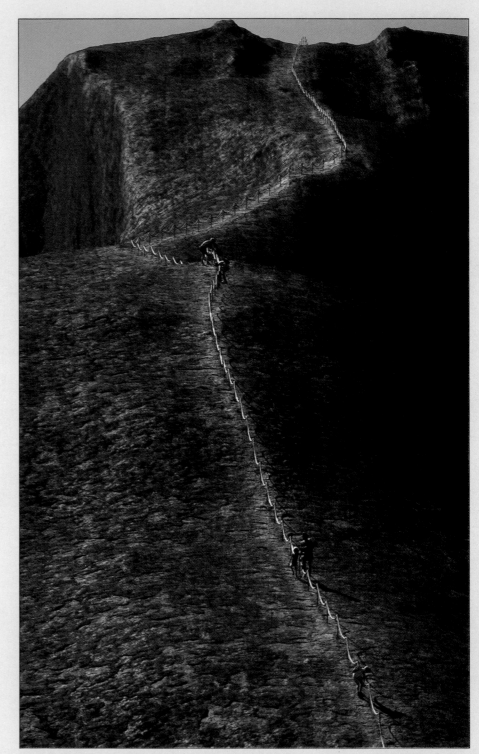

A handrail assists climbers on the rock's western face, the usual point of ascent for visitors.

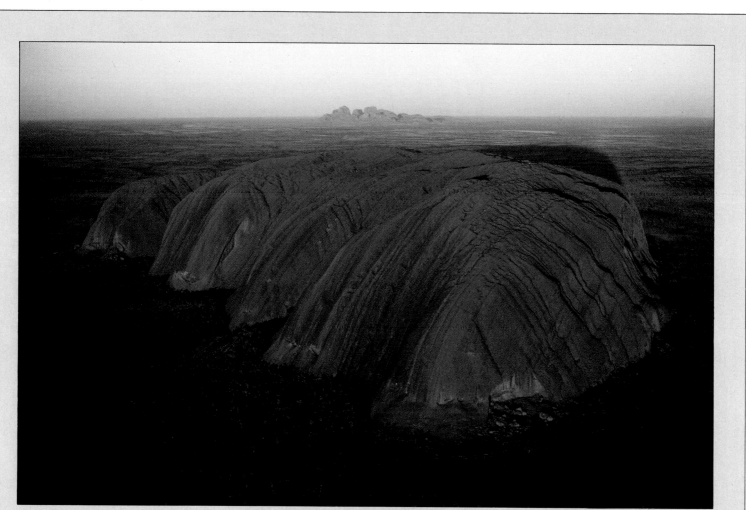

Ayers Rock glows a rich orange in the light of the rising sun. Mount Olga, 20 miles to the west, rises in the background.

In the continent's dry center, Ayers Rock — known to the Aboriginals as Uluru — rises almost sheer from a featureless plain dotted with spinifex grass. Two miles long and five miles in circumference, this vast sandstone monolith shows, iceberg-like, only a small part of its bulk. Though this portion reaches 1,200 feet, the rock outcrop of which it is part extends much farther underground — at least 2,000 feet.

The rock is a geologic rarity. The largest formation of its kind in the world, it is 600 million years old. Soil cannot cling to its rounded back, whose bare stone surface alters color dramatically with the changing light of day. Yet in its hidden crannies, the rock shelters water holes with a rich animal and plant life, making it a vital landmark on Aboriginal trails.

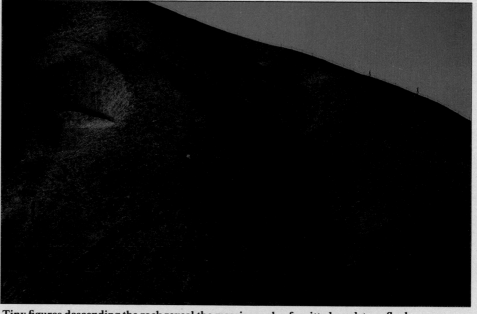

Tiny figures descending the rock reveal the massive scale of a pitted sandstone flank.

ees, for leisure and relaxation. These were sometimes attended by as many as 1,000 members of a tribe, who would come together for dancing and singing, some of the songs being elaborate chants containing several hundred verses that would build up complex word pictures through symbolic allusion and imagery.

There was also a wide repertoire of songs concerned with everyday events. Participants marked the rhythm of the songs by beating together boomerangs, clubs or skin-covered pads; in the north, additional instrumental accompaniment was provided by the didgeridoo, a single-note trumpet fashioned from a hollow sapling or from a section of bamboo with the inner nodes taken out. On informal occasions, an undecorated didgeridoo up to 6½ feet long was used; for ceremonial purposes, the Aboriginals preferred an instrument about 16 feet long and profusely ornamented with designs and feathers.

Different tribes had their own distinctive styles of art, including carved totems, body decoration, and paintings on bark or stone. For paints, they used such natural pigments as yellow or red ocher, pipe clay or charcoal, mixed with water or with the juice of an orchid that acted as a fixative. The paints were applied with a stick, a finger or a feather brush and were often augmented with bird down or fibers that were collected from certain plants.

Most of the Aboriginal paintings had a religious significance, and the artists — always men — either executed traditional designs or created new ones from visions they had seen in dreams. Some works had a sinister significance. If an Aboriginal wished an enemy dead, he commissioned an artist-magician to send the intended victim a death message — usually a simple dot-and-line design burned onto a stick.

At the core of the Aboriginals' world picture was a belief in what they called the Dreamtime, a period when supernatural beings moved over the earth and gave it form and life. The Dreamtime was also a parallel reality in the present, for they further believed that human beings were the descendants of these mythical ancestors and were irrevocably linked to them and the land they had created. Every feature of an Aboriginal's tribal territory — each tree, rock and water hole — contained the spirit of his or her ancestors. Individuals not only knew their way about their land, they also knew its legendary history and its spiritual inhabitants; and because they believed that they were identical with their ancestors, they could feel the land was their own creation; thus any journey meant experiencing not only the comforting presence of the past but also the joy of regeneration.

But the Dreamtime became a nightmare when the white settlers arrived. From the beginning, there were clashes between the Aboriginals and the newcomers. At the time of the dispatch of the First Fleet, the British government had provided high-minded guidelines for the treatment of the king's new Stone Age subjects, and the dutiful Captain Phillip had tried to follow them as best he could. To begin with, he attempted to protect the indigenous population from depredations, even ordering the public flogging of a convict who had stolen some fishing equipment from an Aboriginal tribe. But attempts at an enlightened policy foundered in the great gulf of incomprehension that yawned between the two utterly different societies; the flogging episode, for instance, met with shock and outrage from the tribespeople it was supposed to appease. After a while, maddened by thefts — a concept that was meaningless to the Aboriginals — Phillip was reduced to launching a punitive expedition against them — a concept just as meaningless, and murderous to boot.

Thus the pattern of communication was established. The Aboriginals were regarded as a nuisance, to be driven off into the emptiness with whatever force was needed for the purpose. They had to make way not only for the well-armed Europeans, but for their sheep and cattle too. As settlements proliferated on Australia's coasts and began to expand inland, the continent's original inhabitants were faced with disaster. Casual killings were commonplace and usually went unpunished. The Aboriginals retaliated, demonstrating their skill in guerrilla warfare; but they were outgunned by superior technology and could not put up a sustained resistance. In all Australia's history, probably fewer than 1,000 Europeans were killed by Aboriginals, while at least 10 times as many tribespeople died at the hands of the Europeans.

The fate of the Tasmanian Aboriginals was the worst of all. Their men were butchered for sport, and their women and children were often given to the convicts. In 1804, the year of the first white settlement at Hobart, there may have been as many as 7,000 Aboriginals. By 1824, there were only a few hundred left. In 1831, a somewhat shamefaced government exiled the surviving 190 Aboriginals to an island reservation where, surrounded by the consolations of the Christian religion, they obligingly died out; the last full-blood succumbed in 1876. It is not an episode remembered with pride.

On the mainland, too, Aboriginals were rounded up into missions and reserves, not unlike the reservations established for American Indians. There alcoholism joined illness in drastically reducing their numbers; many died of European diseases, lacking immunity to smallpox or even to common complaints such as measles. Set up mainly between 1900 and 1930, the reserves purportedly offered the Aboriginals protection — in reality, that notion was a euphemism for a policy of segregation. In the state of New South Wales, for example, until 1939, anyone of apparently Aboriginal blood could be forced to live on a reserve under white supervision, and black children were not allowed to attend white schools — which meant that very few Aboriginals received any schooling at all.

In fact, the Aboriginals were very much a nonpeople as far as white Australians were concerned. They were not counted in the census; they were not allowed to vote; they were forbidden to own land; they had to have official permission before they could accept a job, and their wages were paid to the local Protector of Aboriginals — usually a policeman. Those who lived on the reserves were required to do 32 hours of unpaid work each week; defaulters earned themselves a summary punishment of up to two weeks in jail. Insubordination or other offenses could result in an Aboriginal's being sent away to a prison island for an indefinite period of time. Although the officials would never openly admit it, the unspoken assumption that underlay such severe treatment was that the mainland peoples, like their cousins in Tasmania, would quietly die out. As late as 1939, the *Australian Modern Reference Encyclopedia* confidently proclaimed: "The Aborigines, of many tribes, of primitive habits, and a low order of intelligence, are disappearing."

The encyclopedia was wrong. From about the time of World War II, their lot began to improve steadily. First their numbers, long declining, began again to increase. Despite a disturbing rate of infant mortality and short life expectancy, the high birth rates and increasing access to medical services meant that the Aboriginal population started to grow and even to outpace that of the white Australians. In 1971, the first year that the Aboriginals were included in the census, there were estimated to be about 140,000 in the country. By 1976, this figure had been revised upward to 160,000; and in the 1980s, a human-rights report gave the population level as upward of 200,000. It is estimated that by the end of the present century, the number will have reached approximately 300,000 — a significant figure, as it will mean that the population will have returned to the level it had reached before the white settlers arrived in 1788.

Once it was clear that the Aboriginals were not dying out, the policy of confining them to reserves was changed in order to bring them into the economic and social life of the Australian community. The word "assimilation" was widely adopted; in 1951 it was the official strategy of the federal government. The implications were spelled out at a conference of the Commonwealth and State ministers concerned with Aboriginal affairs in 1964: "The policy of assimilation means that all Aborigines and part-Aborigines will attain the same manner of living as other Australians and live as members of a single Australian community enjoying the same rights and privileges, accepting the same responsibilities, observing the same customs and influenced by the same beliefs, hopes and loyalties as other Australians."

This was progress, and the policy of assimilation coincided during the first half of the 1960s with the disappearance of discriminatory laws. Commonwealth legislation that had previously restricted Aboriginal access to social security benefits was amended in 1960, and the electoral rules were changed in 1962 so that adult Aboriginals got the vote. In 1967, the government held a referendum to find out if the Australian population wanted the Aboriginals to be counted in the census and if they wanted the federal government — rather than the state governments, as had been the case — to make laws for the Aboriginals. By a margin of 10 to 1, the vote was in favor on both counts.

However, by this time, critics of the government's policy were complaining

4

that the assimilation program was simply a cover for the destruction of the traditional Aboriginal way of life. Instead, they demanded that the government set up a policy of integration, which would protect the rights of Aboriginals while also leaving them free to follow their own traditions if they chose. The Aboriginals themselves, inspired by the example of minorities in the United States and New Zealand, had started taking militant action to further their aims. The campaign came to focus on land rights.

The first important test case came in 1968, when a group of clans from the Gove Peninsula in the Northern Territory decided to contest the granting of a special mineral lease to a mining company, which intended to quarry bauxite on their territory. Before the case came to court, the prime minister made it clear that their demands would not be acceded to. But when the judge in the case ruled that the Aboriginals held no proprietorial rights to land, even though they had lived on it for generations, the public protest that followed ensured that a change in land-rights law became a major issue in the 1972 election.

The incoming administration appointed a High Court judge to advise on how best the Aboriginals' land rights could be established. He recommended that those living on government reserves should be given nontransferable freehold title and that others should be able to make claims on the basis of tradition to any unalienated Crown land; these proposals were finally passed into law by the succeeding Liberal government of Malcolm Fraser. The Aboriginal Land Rights Act undoubtedly proved the most significant advance in the status of Aboriginals in two centu-

ries. By 1983, 28 percent of the Northern Territory had been given back to them on freehold title, while another 19 percent was under claim; in South Australia and Western Australia, substantial tracts of outback land had been returned to their original owners.

It was the wool trade that originally drove the European settlers into the bush and toward confrontation with the Aboriginals. For more than a century, the nation lived off the sheep's back, with wool providing the nation's main export commodity. Today sheep ranching is still big business, although cattle raising now presents a challenge in terms of the economic activity generated. Taken together, the grazing land for sheep and cattle covers some 1.2 billion acres — more than four times the total area occupied by all the other Australian land use combined. Of this total, sheep stations account for 425 million acres; they are situated chiefly on the southeast and southwest inland plains, where the rainfall averages about 10 inches a year. Cattle stations take up the remaining acres — mainly in northern and central Australia, where the land is too arid for sheep to survive.

Perhaps because of their long pedigree, the owners of the large sheep stations have always occupied a special niche in Australian society, constituting almost an aristocracy. As early as the middle of the 19th century, travelers were observing their resemblance to the landowning families of Britain. A Scot named John Hood, who visited Australia in 1841 to see his squatter son, described such a station: "I have passed a most delightful day at Camden; a more agreeable English-looking place I have not seen. The house, the park, the water, the garden, the style of

everything and of every person, master and servants, resembled so much what one meets with in the old country, that I could scarcely believe myself 16,000 miles from it."

Thirty years later, the English novelist Anthony Trollope, after he had traveled to a lush, well-watered area of the Victoria bush, described ironically how Australian social status and manners were defined by head of sheep: "The number of sheep at these stations will generally indicate with fair accuracy the mode of life at the head stations: 100,000 sheep and upwards require a professed man cook and a butler to look after them; 40,000 sheep cannot be shorn without a piano; 20,000 is the lowest number that renders napkins at dinner imperative; 10,000 require absolute plenty, meat in plenty, tea in plenty, brandy and water and colonial wine in plenty, but do not expect champagne, sherry or made dishes."

Today, the large woolgrowers continue to enjoy a fortunate lifestyle, which is closely modeled on that of the landed gentry in England. Their children are usually educated at private boarding schools. At social events, the young men are distinguishable from their counterparts at county shows in England only by the wide-brimmed felt hats that they wear with their sports coats and twill trousers. All of this is in marked contrast to the rough-and-ready image presented by the small sheep ranchers and by the men who perform all of the manual work on the stations — the shearers, shed hands and roustabouts.

Despite great advances in scientific breeding, the control of diseases and the improvement of pastures, life on Australia's sheep stations has not changed much since the time of the

On a cattle station in the Cloncurry region of Queensland, sunlight catches the wings of a flock of little corellas leaving their roosts at dawn. Members of the cockatoo family, the birds are found in large numbers throughout northern Australia.

squatters. The yearly round is dictated by climate and the rhythm of lambing and shearing; dingoes, rabbits and kangaroos must be controlled, and drought remains a potential killer. Relations within the station are still an ordered hierarchy; wool is pressed and baled by methods similar to those used more than 50 years ago; and the shearing is still carried out by itinerant gangs of skilled workers.

Sheep shearers traditionally were — and to some extent still are — the most respected group of manual workers in the country. When writers began the quest for an Australian national identity in the late 19th century, they elevated these hard-living outback itinerants to the status of folk heroes. Their exploits and way of life were immortalized in bush ballads and in the writings of the two laureates of the outback, Andrew "Banjo" Paterson — whose works include Australia's unofficial anthem, *Waltzing Matilda* — and the poet and short-story writer Henry Lawson.

Shearing was not simply a means of making money; it was a competition, with each man bidding to be the champion, or "ringer," as described in one of Paterson's poems:

The man that rung the Tubbo shed is not the
*   ringer here,*
That stripling from the Coomaside can teach
*   him how to shear.*
They turn away the ragged locks, and rip the
*   cutter goes*
And leaves a track of snowy fleece from bris-
*   ket to the nose;*
It's lovely how they peel it off with never stop
*   nor stay,*
They're racing for the ringer's place this year
*   at Castlereagh.*

Today the wool shearers remain as competitive as ever, but not a single one of the present generation is good enough to challenge Jackie Howe, the most celebrated of all the "guns," as the fast workers are commonly called. In 1802, he established a world record at Alice Downs by shearing 321 sheep in a day, using hand shears.

The other outback workingmen to have become enshrined in the Australian national mythology are the stockmen and the drovers of the cattle stations. Although there were only approximately 34,000 stations in the country in 1980, together they constituted the dominant enterprise over nearly half of all the agricultural land in Australia.

The greatest concentration is in the center and north of the country, areas that, though dry, support native grasses and shrubs that make good cattle fodder. Within this vast semiarid area, where nearly all the water has to be pumped from deep artesian wells, there are stations as large as some countries; properties average more than 500,000 acres in the Northern Territory as a whole, and as much as 1.5 million acres on the Barkly Tableland in the northeastern part of the Northern Territory. Most of these stations are now owned either by Australian meat companies or by British, American or Japanese multinational concerns.

They were originally started, however, by pioneers who followed in the tracks of the outback explorers and sometimes went ahead of them, opening up virgin country on their own initiative. One of the unforeseen benefits to arise from the tragic Burke and Wills expedition of 1860-1861 was that the search parties who went looking for the missing explorers returned with reports of good cattle pasture deep in the outback. Just as, a generation earlier,

sheepmen had moved into the newly opened areas of the southeast, cattlemen began the long trek to the north. At first they concentrated their efforts on the state of Queensland, but by the end of the 1870s, they were searching for new pastures in the northwest.

Reports of good grazing land in the Kimberleys induced Patrick Durack, patriarch of a family of Queensland cattle raisers, to arrange the overland transportation of a mustering of cattle 10,000 strong over a distance of nearly 2,000 miles, from the Cooper Creek area to the Ord River. The leading groups left in May 1883 and did not reach their destination for nearly two and a half years; and, although the journey took a heavy toll of the beasts, there still were sufficient cattle left to found six great properties from which, in years to come, cattle would be sent overland to the southern settlements. But even this great trek fades into insignificance when it is compared with the clearance of cattle from the Northern Territory in 1942, an operation that was organized to deny food to a possible Japanese invasion force. In all, 100,000 head of cattle were moved to the south, and some of them walked a distance of more than 1,000 miles.

In spite of the introduction of new cattle strains and feeds, the sheer size of the northern stations makes careful

The driver of a two-trailer road train *(right)* pauses for a rest while transporting cattle from an outback station to a city slaughterhouse. Long distances and overwhelming heat cause some beasts to die in transit, and they must be disposed of in pits *(above)* before the train reaches its destination.

husbandry, as practiced in more temperate climates, almost impossible. In some areas, the intense heat means that most calves born between dawn and late afternoon will not be able to survive their first day. Not surprisingly, some agronomists have been critical of outback cattle raising, describing it as exploitative and unscientific. One critic writing in the 1960s claimed that there were still stations in the more remote areas of the country where management consisted of two operations: branding cattle in order to establish ownership and "turning off" — shipping out for sale — those cattle that could be rounded up.

Outback cattle are still kept on undeveloped pasture, and when drought reduces the amount of natural fodder and the carrying capacity of the land, there is a race to round up the herd and get the cattle to market before they die of starvation or grow too thin to bring a reasonable price. The problem lies in gathering the wild cattle that roam in the stations' outer limits. In the past, mounted stockmen would track them down, manually wrestle them to the ground, then lash their hind legs together with a rope or leather strap. "Coaches" — tractable cattle from the home pastures — would be driven up to the hobbled beast. Calmed by their docile presence, the wild bull or cow would then be untied and driven back to the stock camp. Nowadays, however, aircraft are often used in rounding up the herds. Several fixed-wing airplanes, perhaps augmented by a helicopter, may help to drive the cattle into a fenced area set up at the end of a long funnel constructed from burlap or other natural materials.

Until the 1960s, cattle were driven to market or a railroad terminal by drovers — tough men whose reputation for rough camaraderie and drinking perhaps exceeded even that of the sheep shearers:

Now there's a trade you all know well,
It's bringing cattle over;
I'll tell you all about the time
When I became a drover.
I made a line for Queensland,
To Kempsey I did wander;
I picked up a mob of duffers there
And began as an overlander.

4

High living was the order of the day once the cattle had been sold and the drovers had been paid their wages:

In town we drain the whisky glass
And go to see the play;
We never think of being hard up
Or how to spend the day;
We sheer up to the pretty girls
Who rig themselves with grandeur,
And as long as we spend our check, my lads,
They love the overlander.

The heirs of the overlanders are the drivers of the road trains — monsters of the road, each consisting of a mammoth truck towing as many as four trailers like freight cars on tires. Even with only two trailers, a road train may be up to 200 feet long and carry 100 cattle or 600 sheep. Meeting a road train on a lonely outback highway is an extremely nerve-racking experience, especially at night, when the first indication of the impending giant is just a distant glow on the horizon from the truck's giant headlights. With infinite slowness the glow will become larger and brighter, and the noise of the engine will gradually make itself heard. Finally, the long train will roar past with a rush of air strong enough to jostle the suspension of the sturdiest car, before the trailers behind it, illuminated with strings of lights, fall away into the darkness, rising and falling with the surface of the road like some great primeval beast.

Unwelcoming at the best of times, the outback can in extreme circumstances prove a lethal enemy. Its dangers are graphically illustrated by the story of

A pregnant Aboriginal woman (below) receives medical attention aboard one of the Flying Doctor Service's 28 airplanes. Operating from 14 bases, the planes can be summoned by radio to airlift patients needing treatment from sheep- and cattle-station landing strips (right) to hospitals.

Harry Lasseter who, one day in March 1930, presented himself in the office of John Bailey, President of the Australian Worker's Union. He had a startling tale to tell. Twenty-three years earlier, he said, he had found a vein of gold while searching for rubies in the mountains of central Australia; seeking to return with his spoils, he had gotten lost, and his horses had perished one by one. He had been rescued by a surveyor named Harding, with whom he subsequently returned in search of the lost vein of gold. They relocated it, and this time Lasseter marked its position; but when they returned to civilization, they found that their watches were running slow and consequently the bearings they had taken were incorrect. In the following years, gold was discovered in other, easier areas of the outback and, Lasseter said, he himself had joined in one of the rushes. He had temporarily

put aside further plans to revisit the area of his earlier find, although he continued to nurture dreams of its eventual rediscovery.

There was a certain vagueness about Lasseter's account that did not inspire much confidence, and many people have subsequently questioned whether there was any truth in it at all. But in 1930, in John Bailey's office, his story fell on appreciative ears. The other gold fields had been mined out, and the Great Depression was beginning to be felt. Whatever misgivings had been expressed, a consortium of Sydney businessmen was found to provide financial backing for a new sortie in search of the gold, and a company was established to organize the quest. Funds were not lacking. When the six-man party at last set out from Alice Springs, it could call on the services of a specially designed six-wheeled truck, an auxiliary truck

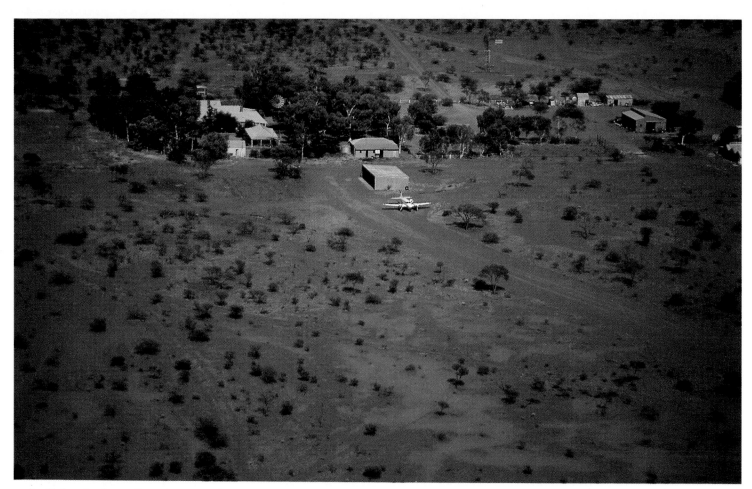

and a light airplane. In contrast to Lasseter's earlier, amateur efforts, this was the best-equipped expedition in the history of Australian mineral exploration to that time.

Whether or not Lasseter lied in his original claims, it is certain that the later quest became an epic of endurance. The story of the next five months' adventures is a catalogue of extravagant misfortune that will seem astonishing only to those who are unfamiliar with outback travel. The airplane crashed on take-off on its second flight. A replacement sent out by the company directors made one successful reconnaissance, in the course of which Lasseter claimed to recognize landmarks near the site. It then returned to the coast,

the pilots refusing to make any further sorties over such dangerous territory without the security of a larger engine and fuel tank. The six-wheeled truck was forced to turn back when it reached an impassable stretch of sandstone country scored by ledges as much as 300 feet deep. Lasseter, whose obsession with finding gold was matched only by his mistrust of his traveling companions, persuaded them to return to Alice Springs. Then he pressed forward in the company of a young bushman called Paul Johns, who had attached himself to the party. Food and equipment were carried on Johns's five camels; but as the train arrived at the Petermann Ranges — the goal of the quest — unexpected rain swiftly turned

the desert into a quagmire, bogging down the beasts of burden. Even without this unexpected setback, Lasseter seems to have made up his mind not to let Johns see the gold. Irrationally, he insisted on turning back. The two men came to blows, but Lasseter was adamant. Retracing their steps, they journeyed 120 miles to their base camp, and Lasseter, taking just two of the camels, set off again, this time on his own.

The rest of his story is known only from Aboriginal oral history and from fragmentary and heat-damaged journals and letters, buried by the prospector in caves where he had taken shelter and underneath the ashes of his campfires. He returned to the Petermanns and rediscovered the vein of gold. He

4

pegged it, marking his claim to the gold; but before he left the site to reestablish contact with his companions and the wider world, disaster struck. As he started to unload the camels for the night's camp, the beasts bolted. They disappeared over the horizon, leaving Lasseter alone in the desert with a revolver and perhaps a fortnight's supply of food, but no water. He was discovered by a wandering group of Pitjantjatjara Aboriginals. He traveled with them for a month or more; but relations between the tribespeople and their uninvited guest were always somewhat edgy, and Lasseter's journals speak of attempts on his life as well as acts of individual kindness.

Matters came to a head when the tribe encamped for several weeks in a well-watered valley. Lasseter's plight had steadily worsened. He had been struck down by dysentery and a form of conjunctivitis known in the bush as sandy blight. He also learned, through the Aboriginals' bush telegraph of smoke signals, that the airplanes he expected to be searching the area for him had not been sighted. Alone, scared, sick and sheltering in a cave, he made the mistake of shooting at some Aboriginal youths he thought had come to taunt him. Some of the tribal elders, already unsettled by his presence, then "sang" him, which meant they had cast a fatal curse. Regarding him to all intents and purposes as already dead, they withdrew all material support. Starvation threatened.

By now, Lasseter's sufferings were intense. His waistline had shrunk so much that he had taken in his belt by 10 notches. He was tormented by flies and ants, which, he wrote, "have nearly eaten my face away." He had virtually lost the use of both eyes. In this condition,

he set off with a quart and a half of water — the most he could carry in his weakened state — to try to cover the 80 miles to Mount Olga, where he hoped help would be waiting. He never got there. It was just 33 miles from the cave to where his bones were discovered by the relief party.

Subsequently, several expeditions tried to retrace Lasseter's tracks in the Petermanns, but none met with success. If he was telling the truth, then somewhere in the dry mountains, undisturbed by all the mineral exploration activity of the postwar years, his gold vein still waits to be rediscovered.

Lasseter's story indicates vividly the difficulties and dangers of mineral exploration in the outback, especially for those foolhardy enough to try going it alone. Yet the rewards in many cases have been more than commensurate with the efforts involved. Scattered through the Australian hinterland are such successful and long-established mining centers as the opal fields of Coober Pedy; the lead, zinc and silver

mines at Broken Hill in New South Wales; and Kalgoorlie in Western Australia, once the scene of a famous gold rush and again in the 1980s a major center for the mineral.

The mineral boom of the postwar years brought a new breed to the outback. It was pioneered less by the prospectors of the old school than by university-trained geologists, whose educated guesses, supported by full-scale surveys financed by mining companies, proved right often enough to encourage the belief that Australia's remote inland might be an unexploited treasure house. The long list of their successes includes many different natural resources — from iron ore, nickel and bauxite in Western Australia, through copper, uranium, iron and petroleum in the Northern Territory, to uranium, lead, zinc, silver, gas and bauxite in Queensland. Yet the harsh rules of outback living have not changed, despite the influx of all the up-to-date technology; accounts of mining workers meeting their death when they stroll out of the protected environment of the camp and lose their way still appear with tragic frequency in Australian newspapers.

The outback's other great resource is empty space, an asset most spectacularly tapped by the rocket range that stretches for thousands of miles from Woomera in South Australia to the Indian Ocean coastline south of Broome. For much of the distance, this vast testing ground passes over totally uninhabited desert, flat and open enough for scientists to have little difficulty in tracking down strayed missiles and lost parts by taking sight checks from the air. Those few sheep stations that lie within the range's edges were thoughtfully provided with concrete shelters by the Australian government, which shared the cost of constructing the range with Britain. The missile testing and satellite tracking carried out from the range have mercifully not required the shelters to be used; so far they have seen service only as supplementary farm buildings. More recently, the Australian government has joined with the United States government to run defense bases whose functions are to monitor missile launches and nuclear explosions and to provide a military early warning system; one of these lies in the heart of the outback at Pine Gap, 16 miles southwest of Alice Springs.

The social infrastructure that links the widely scattered population of the outback is necessarily limited by the great distances involved, but it includes two unique features developed to conquer the problems of remoteness: the Flying Doctor Service and the School of the Air. Each is an attempt to bring basic social services to citizens who may live as much as 900 miles from the nearest city and hundreds of miles from the closest hospital or school. Until well into the 20th century, most of the outback children were educated by their parents or were self-taught, and commonplace illnesses such as appendicitis were often fatal, since it took days and sometimes weeks to get medical aid.

It was to cope with situations such as this, and to help the people of the outback to communicate with their neighbors, that the Reverend John Flynn set up the Flying Doctor Service. Ordained as a Presbyterian minister in 1911, Flynn had experienced for himself the isolation of the settlers when he traveled on missionary work in the bush. With the help of his church and other missionaries, he established a small hos-

pital, staffed with nurses, at Oodnadatta in South Australia in 1912. It proved so successful that he received many requests to build others. Since the construction and operating costs were prohibitive, Flynn set out to provide medical aid for people in the bush with the help of airplanes.

The idea of using aircraft to solve the problem came from a young medical student named Clifford Peel, who outlined his plan to Flynn shortly before going off to fight in World War I as a pilot with the Australian Flying Corps. Peel was killed in action before his idea became reality. In fact, it took until 1928 to inaugurate the service — a delay caused by the need to raise money and develop a rudimentary radio network that would link up the outlying homesteads. Money was eventually raised by donation; the communications problem was solved by an amateur radio enthusiast who developed a bicycle-powered Morse code transmitter. By 1929, the first six sets were in-

stalled on properties within a 300-mile radius of the service's first headquarters, at Cloncurry in Queensland. The users could receive spoken messages from the radio station, but they had to send their replies in Morse code, producing the necessary power by operating a pedal-driven generator.

By this time, Flynn had recruited his first doctor, a surgeon from Sydney who, in the inaugural year, flew almost 17,000 miles in a deHavilland biplane, answering about 250 emergency calls. The service was an immediate success and rapidly expanded. By the 1980s, it had grown into a nationwide network of 14 bases equipped with 28 hospital airplanes and employing a staff of more than 100. In 1981, the service transported more than 9,000 patients on evacuation and repatriation flights; most of them were Aboriginals.

To simplify the administration, non-emergency calls from the homesteads are received at scheduled times; they are then transmitted via the radio sta-

4

tion to a hospital, where a doctor and a nurse diagnose the symptoms. After diagnosis, the doctor prescribes a course of do-it-yourself treatment or, if necessary, arranges for the patient to be evacuated for hospital care. To facilitate treatment, each station linked to the Flying Doctor network is equipped with a comprehensive medical kit that has each item numbered for identification. The doctor simply tells the caller what number medicine to use and how to administer it.

The School of the Air began in 1950 under the aegis of the older service, and it used the two-way radio transmitter and receiver at the Flying Doctor base in Alice Springs. Three decades later, it was a well-organized program, receiving funds from state governments and broadcasting to some 20,000 pupils scattered over almost 900,000 square miles. Teachers speak simultaneously over two channels, to ensure good reception at homesteads both near and far. Each time they ask a question, the pupils competing to get their answer in first may live as much as 900 miles apart. Once a year, largely at the school's expense, the children are brought together to meet their teachers. Primary-school-age children rendezvous in Alice Springs; older pupils gather in one of the large cities, thereby broadening their experience of Australia and the world, as well as learning to match the faces with the voices that have become so familiar to them in the course of the preceding 12 months.

Other social events in the outback's calendar are few and far between. There are race meetings for amateur jockeys — the most famous is held each June at Brunette Downs in the Northern Territory — and rodeos in country towns or on the large cattle stations.

Popular sports at these rough-and-ready agricultural shows include steer riding, judged on the length of time each contestant can stay on the bucking animal; buckjumping, in which unbroken stallions take the place of the steers; and camp drafting, which involves racing to round up small groups of cattle. But the most keenly followed activity is wood chopping, in which the competitors chop and saw through timber logs, using axes so finely honed that they could probably shave with them.

In Darwin, there is an annual regatta for rafts made out of empty beer cans, always in plentiful supply in that thirsty northern metropolis. But the event that best sums up the spirit of the outback in all its dry irony is held in Alice Springs. It is whimsically known as the Henley-on-Todds regatta — "Henley" from the celebrated boating center on England's River Thames, "Todd" from Alice's own river. The joke is that this river is almost always dry; the water course fills only after rare heavy rainfall. To complete the irony, the organizers each year take out insurance against rain, for water would spoil the whole purpose of the event, which is for competing teams to run along the bed of the river in yachts that have no bottoms. Alternatively, sculls race along rails, propelled by rowers digging their oars into sand. This preposterous and energetically pursued exercise has now become a major tourist attraction, and it draws visitors not just from the outback itself but also from the southern cities. In its unpretentious way, it says a great deal about the manner in which the people of Australia have come to terms with the harsh and unforgiving hinterland of their country — not with fear and not with awe so much as with a dry and stoic humor. □

A helicopter, used to round up cattle from the hills, hovers in swirling dust over several thousand animals waiting to be driven to the stockyards.

AN ABORIGINAL REVIVAL

Sole occupants of the Australian continent for tens of thousands of years, the Aboriginals came close to extinction within a century of the arrival of European settlers. Their numbers declined, they were driven from their traditional lands, and their lifestyle was largely destroyed. Over the past decades, however, their fortunes have revived: The population is now rising, and legislation has restored at least some of their territory.

Symptomatic of the new, optimistic mood is the "outstation" movement. Several hundred clans, mainly in Western Australia and the Northern Territory, have formed tribal communities that live as much as possible in the traditional manner. No longer nomadic, they accept such compromises as the need to herd some livestock and make handcrafts for sale. But as these pictures — taken on Arnhem Land outstations — show, they continue to practice their old hunting skills and preserve their culture through painting, dance and song.

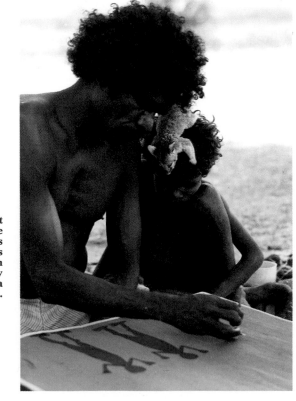

Watched by his son and a lively pet possum, the Aboriginal artist George Milpurrur paints an event from his clan's history on a strip of eucalyptus bark. His colors are made from such natural materials as ground ocher, clay and charcoal and are applied with a soft twig, which serves as a brush.

A detail of a much larger painting by
Milpurrur shows clan ancestors meeting animals from the Dreamtime — the
legendary period when the world was
made. Bark paintings by leading artists
command high prices among city
collectors, providing a valuable source
of revenue for some outstations.

Walking into a breeze to keep the flames behind him, a spear-carrying man lights dry undergrowth with a firebrand of rolled bark. Setting controlled fires to burn off scrub is a vital safety measure in the dry season, when hunters could be trapped by accidental conflagrations.

Large strips of bark draped over a framework of branches make a house big enough for several families to share. In the past, when Aboriginals were nomadic, they built only temporary shelters. Today's stations are permanent settlements, and the houses are used all year long.

A family on the Yathalamarra station tends pumpkins, zucchini and onions in a garden partly sheltered from the fierce sun by trees. Traditionally, Aboriginals gathered only wild plants as vegetables, but crop-growing has been adopted by some out-stations as an additional food source.

125

Carrying her son on her shoulders, a woman from the Nangala outstation walks home from a fresh-water swamp with the proceeds of a morning's food-gathering: a long-necked turtle and two water lilies. The turtle will be roasted over hot stones, gutted and cut in-to chunks; the lilies will be eaten raw.

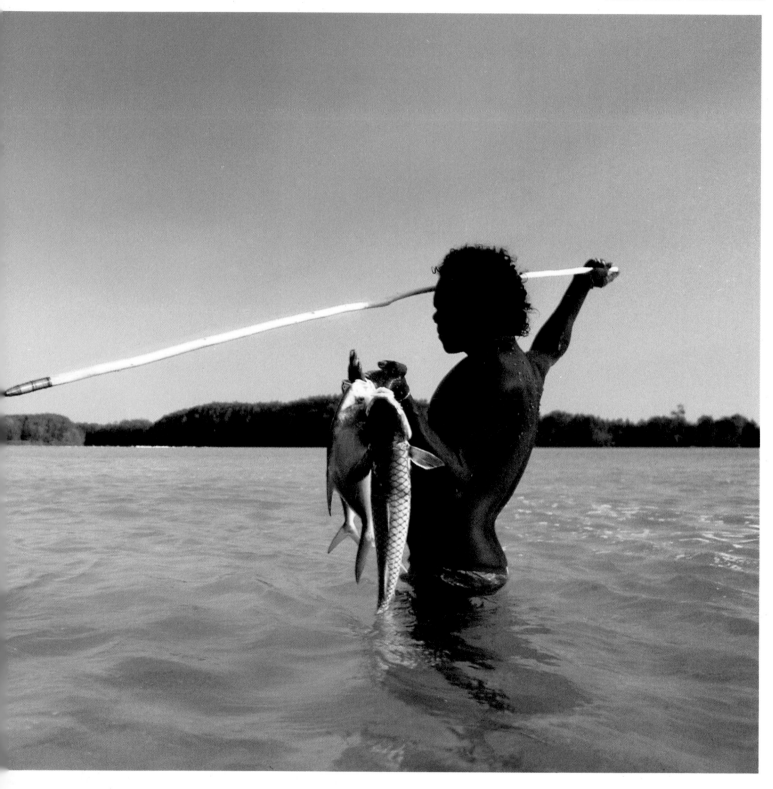

Near Maningrida, a man fishing in the open sea uses a traditional pronged spear to increase his catch, so far consisting of two flat moonfish and a large mullet. Fish are plentiful off the Arnhem Land coast, but catching them requires courage, because the waters are infested with crocodiles.

To the deep, droning notes of the didgeridoo — a hollowed-out tree trunk played as a musical instrument — Aboriginals in the Roper Valley perform dances passed down through generations. The participants may imitate animal movements, as in the kangaroo dance *(below)*, or reenact tribal rites from the distant past in spear dances *(right)*. Such secular dances have always played an important part in corroborees — or ceremonial gatherings. Aboriginal men also practice other, sacred dances never seen in public — or by the women of the clan.

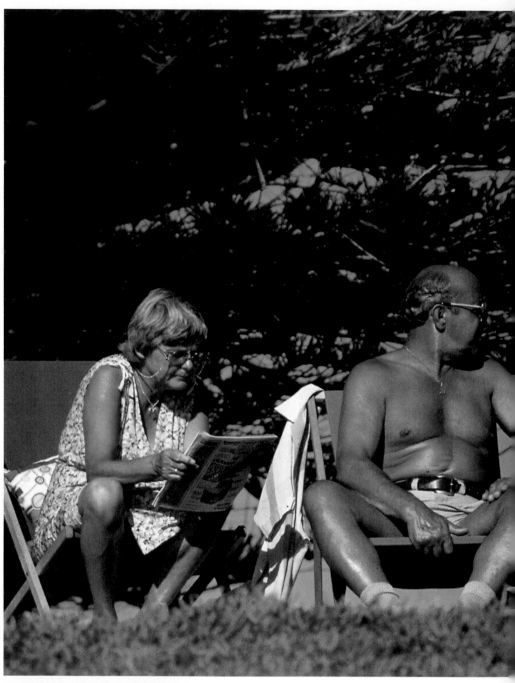

A couple relaxes in deck chairs in a
Perth park while a swimsuit-clad woman lies in sun-soaked oblivion behind
them. A sunny climate has made Australians an outdoor people, as enthusiastic about the noncompetitive pleasures of sun-bathing as about sports.

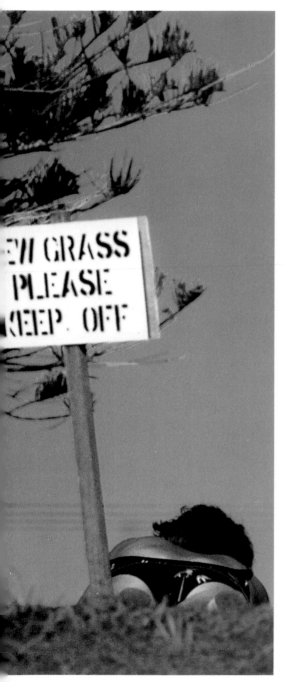

PLEASURE AS A WAY OF LIFE

Australians enjoy more leisure time than their counterparts in most other countries. In addition to the four to five weeks' paid vacation that the average worker expects each year, there are about a dozen official holidays, which are usually scheduled for Mondays so that employees can look forward to three-day weekends. Then there is that other national institution, the "sickie" — a sick day, which has been regularized in some occupations to the point that people take the maximum number of permitted days a year. It is amazing how often the "sickie" turns out to coincide with the midweek horse races, or with an important Test (international) cricket match or the Melbourne Cup horse race. All these official and unofficial holidays act as relief valves from the monotony and pressures of modern full-time work, and though they might be the despair of economists and business leaders, they are regarded by most Australians as inalienable rights.

The recreation patterns have been changing recently for the beneficiaries of these generous amounts of spare time. In the past, public leisure activities tended to be male-oriented, gregarious and focused on spectator sports, drinking and betting on "the dogs, the trots and the races" — greyhound racing, trotting and conventional horse racing. Now, however, participation is the major theme. Instead of herding as anonymous spectators into some huge

sports crowd, Australians are more likely to jump into cars on a weekend and fan out to a variety of more individual pursuits: a day spent at the beach, bush picnics, camping, maybe some sailing or surfing, a party at night or a visit to the local beer garden on Sunday "arvo," meaning "afternoon."

The new leisure pattern is also less masculine in emphasis. The trend is evident in sports: Nearly every activity, from auto racing and wrestling to soccer, is now open to women. Women have gained admittance to that bastion of masculinity, the surf lifesaving club, and have forced their way into the jockey clubs. But the most dramatic invasion of a traditional male preserve has taken place in the taverns and bars of the nation. Once, drinking was an almost all-male activity; the pubs used to be crowded with shouting, swearing, " 'ave another beer, mate" drinkers, and they exuded what the British travel writer Jan Morris described as "a frightening sense of male collusion." Women were banned from the bars or consigned to sit in dowdy little ladies' lounges at the back of the pub. There are still a few "bloodhouses," as the rowdier institutions are called, patronized exclusively by men; but these days women drink wherever they please, and the typical pub has carpeted barrooms, an entertainment lounge and an open-air beer garden where men and women drink together.

Approximately 64 percent of women

and 83 percent of men in Australia consume alcohol, and for both sexes, beer is still the most popular brew. Drinking habits, though, have mellowed somewhat. Australians used to boast about how strong their beer was, but in the mid-1980s, there was a major shift in the market to low-alcohol beers — a move perhaps encouraged by the introduction of random blood-alcohol tests on motorists by the police.

At the same time, there has been an astonishing growth in the consumption of Australian wines. Once dismissed by the experts as "plonk," the vintages of the Barossa and Clare valleys in South Australia, the Hunger Valley in New South Wales and other vinicultural centers have gained an international reputation, and every bar and drive-in liquor store has wine for sale in a variety of sizes. Virtually all the newspapers — even the afternoon tabloids — have their own wine columnists, while magazines, such as the *National Times,* carry wine supplements, wine guides and pages of advertisements.

The increasing affluence of the postwar era has created a surge of enthusiasm for new and expensive outdoor activities, especially such water sports as skin diving, water-skiing, yachting and motorboating. On weekends, Sydney Harbor is crammed with yachts and craft of every conceivable shape and size; and the lakes and estuaries of the coast have all kinds of mooring, from backyard piers to marinas where, because of the lack of space at sea level, the boats have to be stacked like trays by fork-lift trucks in open, multistory warehouses. Windsurfing and hanggliding have also become popular. The most exclusive outdoor activity is skiing, which even well-paid middle-class Australians find expensive, despite the fact — touted by tourist brochures — that the Snowy Mountains have more usable snowfields than Switzerland.

The change in the economics of leisure is noticeable in many other areas. People in their teens and twenties have high enough salaries to pay substantial sums for tickets to see the world's top rock bands and entertainers. One of the major arenas for such events is the circular 20,000-capacity Sydney Entertainment Center, built by the New South Wales Labor government and the most important new public building in the city since the construction of the Sydney Opera House.

The new wealth is visible even on the streets — for example, in the number of ordinary family cars that are equipped with towbars to haul a camper, van, boat or trail bike around the countryside. Off-road driving has become popular, with sales of four-wheel-drive vehicles soaring and most suburban streets adorned with at least one wide-wheeled, multistriped, imported Land Cruiser, Prairie, Jackaroo, Patrol Wagon or Range Rover. A lot of them never leave the asphalt, of course; but they look as though they could if the owners

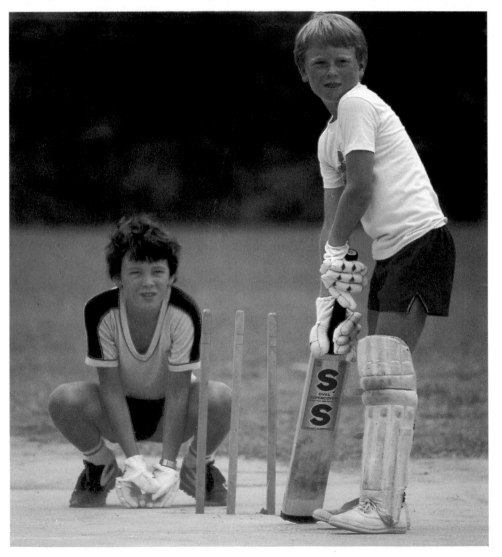

Correctly padded and gloved for a casual afternoon cricket match, a young batsman takes guard in front of a watchful wicket keeper. Cricket is an early enthusiasm for many Australians and is played very seriously even at the elementary-school level.

were willing to risk damaging the installment-bought vehicles. Even more in evidence are the private swimming pools that grace 1 in 10 Australian homes. To take the work out of pool cleaning, an Australian team invented the world's first automatic cleaner, the "creepy crawly," which moves over the pool floor and sucks up grime and dirt.

Other elements of Australian leisure have remained constant. Visiting the homes of friends and relatives, often unannounced, just to "have a chat" is a confirmed habit; Australians will happily drive miles to see the family or to attend a party. In some country areas, an old social custom is still practiced: The men gather together at one end of the room, telling tales around a keg of beer, while the women chat among themselves at the other. In the cities and larger towns, however, there is no segregation, and a freewheeling sexuality is apparent. Australia has cast off most of its notorious puritanism, which once made the "wowser," or killjoy, a familiar figure in public life; the nation now has porn shops, R-rated movies, a plethora of sex magazines — including women's magazines with nude male centerfolds — and some of the most straightforwardly sexual television advertising in the world.

Gambling is also as prevalent as ever, although the forms it takes have

THE BIG RACE

On the first Tuesday of each November, some 80,000 people crowd into Flemington Race Course for the country's most prestigious horse race, the Melbourne Cup. Initiated in 1861, the two-mile classic provides an opportunity for displays of race-course elegance as well as for resolute betting. Off the track it brings the nation to a temporary halt, as the High Court goes into recess, Parliament stops its debates, and an estimated third of the nation tunes in to follow the action on radio or television.

With the city skyline in the background, jockeys gallop home in the Melbourne Cup.

A row of well-dressed women display decorum in the members' enclosure at Flemington.

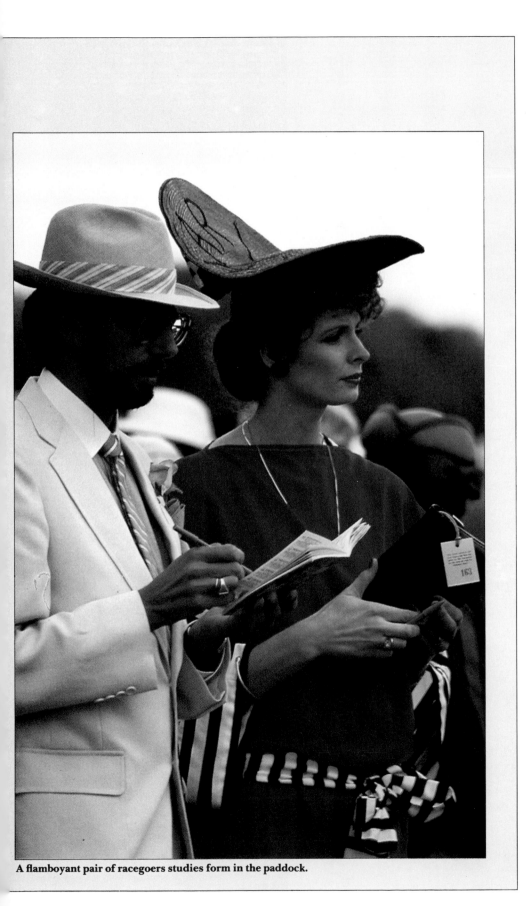

A flamboyant pair of racegoers studies form in the paddock.

changed. Australians, it is claimed, are the heaviest gamblers in the world and will bet on flies crawling up a window-pane. The state governments, under whose legislation gambling falls, foster rather than discourage the compulsion. They have introduced variations of Lotto, such as Scratch Lotto — a form of the game in which the numbers on the card are revealed when opaque coatings are scratched away — in addition to the old state-run lotteries. They also run off-track betting through totalisator agencies (the "tote," a mechanical device that shows the number of bets placed on a race and divides the winnings equally, is an Australian invention). Casinos, which once were banned throughout the continent, have been introduced legally at places like West Point in Tasmania and illegally in the baccarat clubs and gaming houses of Melbourne and Sydney, which survive only because the authorities choose to look the other way.

Slot machines — called one-armed bandits — were banned in the states of Victoria and Queensland, but in New South Wales they form the financial backbone of the huge sports and "rissole" — RSL, or Returned Servicemen's League — social clubs. These popular institutions, which are now open to virtually anyone who wishes to become a member, often boast bars, restaurants, game rooms, dance floors and "pokies." Playing the pokies, or slot machines, is an obsession that cuts across gender, generation and class; in the clubs, which have replaced pubs as the primary gathering places in many suburbs and towns, the rows of one-armed bandits are often attended by battalions of people who — with cigarettes dangling from their mouths and beers in hand — spend hours feeding

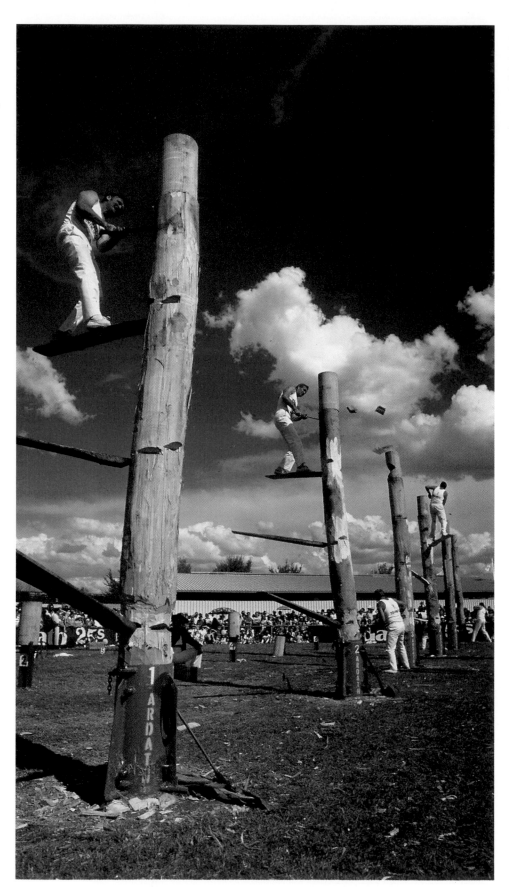

During a wood-chopping contest in Canberra, brawny axmen race to cut through upright logs. Starting at the top, contestants move down one plank each time they cut through a section of timber. The winner is the first to reach the ground.

change into the insatiable machines.

In the face of stiff competition from the pokies, Australia's traditional gambling game, Two-up, is dying out. Besides, because of betting abuses in the past, it is illegal. To play the game, people surround a central spinner and bet on whether two pennies, spun from a flat piece of wood called the kip, will turn up heads or tails; if the coins are unmatched, the spinner then keeps the stakes. Today, Two-up survives mainly in army camps and as a nostalgic diversion among ex-servicemen on Anzac Day. Many more people gamble on horse racing, even though they may never visit a race track; a poll taken in the 1970s concluded that 1 out of 6 Australians bet on the horses at least once a month and an additional 1 in 4 had an occasional flutter.

Although the pubs and clubs are the most popular places to spend an evening out, nighttime leisure, as in most Western countries, is dominated by television. According to surveys, nearly all Australian families own a television set; 7 out of 10 Australians watch TV programs regularly; and 3 in 10 watch almost every night. Almost every home has a radio, and the advent of the "trannie," or portable radio, and portable cassette player has resulted in great numbers of young Australians carrying their music with them wherever they go. This has, in turn, prompted a rash of new antinoise ordinances.

Then there are such predominantly nighttime pursuits as going to the movies and dancing. But in this area as well, there has been a move from the communal to the domestic. Australians have taken to home-video cassettes with a vengeance; video parties are all the rage, and almost every suburb, town and village in the nation sports a videocassette rental shop. As a result, movie audiences are getting smaller and smaller, while the once-popular drive-ins are closing down everywhere because of the lack of customers. The old-time dance hall has also disappeared, and it has been replaced by discotheques, clubs and live-music nightspots, where young people tend to dance alone rather than with somebody; even if they have partners, they perform separately, facing the band rather than each other.

For weekends and holidays, Australians love to "get away from it all." Some 80 percent of Australians spend their vacations away from home. The majority stays in Australia, usually traveling by car and staying in motels, campgrounds or campers, or else with friends or family. A predominantly urban people, Australians like getting out into the bush, and a Sunday-afternoon drive, followed by a bush picnic, is almost a national institution.

For energetic hikers, there are splendid national parks and state forests along the coastline and scattered throughout the interior. Most have campsites, which may be booked up months in advance, especially for Easter and other major holidays. The distances involved do not deter vacationers; it is common for Sydneysiders to make the overnight drive of about 600 miles in order to reach the Gold Coast beaches of Queensland, or to drive 270 miles to the Snowy Mountains trout streams for a weekend of fishing. Many Australians own "weekenders" — vacation homes — on the coast or out in the bush.

The same readiness to travel for pleasure can be seen in the extraordinary number of Australians who take holidays overseas: nearly one million a

year, according to the Australian Bureau of Statistics. For their vacations, some of them travel to places such as Bali, which is, in fact, closer for Western Australians to visit than the east coast of their own country. Package tours to the Pacific islands, the Philippines and Hong Kong are often a better bargain than flights from the southern cities to the vacation resorts of Queensland. Large numbers of Australians also make the Grand Tour of Britain and Europe. Certain streets in London are lined with secondhand campers offered for sale by Australian owners seeking to raise the price of the air fare home; and along Europe's hitchhiking routes, backpackers sporting the Australian flag are a regular part of the scenery.

The appeal of globe-trotting for the young Australians shows no sign of abating. A prolonged period of foreign travel is a once-in-a-lifetime initiation rite for many high-school and university graduates before they settle down to start careers and families. Others choose to save their money so they will be able to travel after several years of working, seeking something other than their comfortable, basically insular world. If Australia has become more cosmopolitan and more sophisticated over the years, then part of the reason is the breakdown of the geographic loneliness that once condemned Australian culture to parochialism.

In one field at least, the charge of parochialism has never been applicable. Considering the small population of Australia, its record in international sports is little short of astonishing. For years, Australia was the pacesetter in world-class swimming, and it has an almost unrivaled record in tennis. The

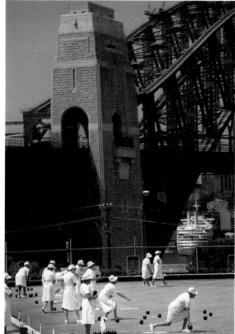

nation won the Davis Cup — the premier international team event in tennis — 19 times between 1939 and 1983 and produced 37 Wimbledon champions, including doubles partners, up to 1982. The roll call of stars includes John Bromwich, Lew Hoad, Ken Rosewell, Rod Laver, John Newcombe, Margaret Court and the part-Aboriginal Evonne Cawley, née Goolagong.

Australia is also one of the world's great cricketing nations. It has won the Ashes, as the England-Australia Test match series is known, as many times as England, from whom it learned the game; and in Don Bradman, it produced probably the finest batsman the game has ever known. It has had world champions in auto racing, squash, horseback riding, shooting, track and boxing. In the early 1980s, it led the world in Rugby League soccer and

TRADITIONS OF BRAWN AND BRAVERY

Lifesavers carrying life lines march in the opening parade of the annual Sydney surf carnival.

Through the height of the Australian summer, the nation's 236 surf lifesaving clubs — bands of volunteer lifeguards organized to help swimmers and surfers in distress — hold a colorful series of weekend carnivals along the coast. Those held on the beaches of Sydney are the most famous, attracting large crowds with their unique pageantry and their thrilling displays of split-second teamwork.

Each carnival begins with a parade in which the lifesavers bear their club banners. Then there are staged rescue and resuscitation exercises, judged on speed of execution. But for the spectators, the high point of the day is usually the surfboat races, in which crews in row boats compete furiously against one another and the waves to round marker buoys beyond the surf line and return to shore.

Competing in the surfboat race, a crew of five struggles to pull its craft through the pounding breakers to a distant marker buoy.

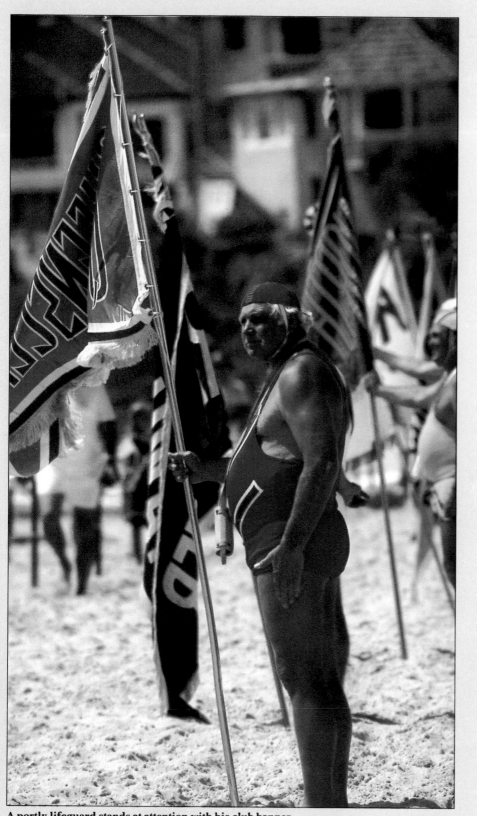
A portly lifeguard stands at attention with his club banner.

surfing, and in 1983 it won the world's most coveted yachting prize, the America's Cup, which the United States had held for 132 years. No other country of similar population can boast such an impressive sports record.

The stars who have managed to put Australia on the sports map are the product of a long-standing national sports tradition that, at any one time, involves literally millions of ordinary Australians. A series of Gallup polls conducted shortly after World War II discovered that about 4 out of 10 Australians regularly participated in a sport, and 3 out of 4 were spectators. In schools, children still take such an interest in games that teachers sometimes have to discourage them from becoming obsessive.

The nation is, of course, blessed with an ideal climate and environment for physical exercise. The Australians can swim in the ocean nearly all year round, except in Tasmania and perhaps Victoria, where the wearing of wetsuits is a necessity in the colder months for aficionados of surfing and wind-surfing. In such a sparsely settled continent, there is plenty of space for outdoor pursuits, and the long, warm summers enable people to indulge their love of outdoor sports as much as they like. The aridity of the interior is a drawback, but most country towns have an Olympic-size swimming pool. They may also have such things as an 18-hole golf course, a race track, fair grounds, showground, several cricket and soccer fields, tennis courts, squash courts, indoor gymnasiums, a greyhound and trotting track, a speedway, roads with special bicycle lanes, walking trails, a roller-skating rink and a shooting range. In the cities, these facilities are augmented by places that cater to the

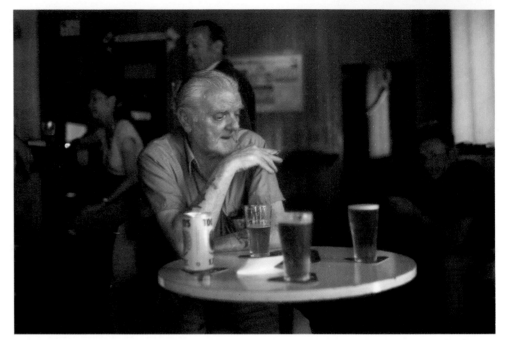

latest products of the physical-fitness craze — jazz exercise, yoga, martial arts, saunas, bodybuilding. Some of the health and exercise clubs are situated on the top floor of city buildings so that busy executives can have a workout in the middle of the day, followed by lunch at a health-food restaurant attached to the club.

While the trend is toward individual participation, traditional spectator sports, such as cricket and soccer, still generate tremendous interest. Since the 1970s, they have become heavily commercialized. Rugby League players and even referees have the names of sponsors on the backs of their jerseys, and soccer fields are festooned with advertisements for cigarettes. Cricket resisted the grosser aspects of commercialism until 1977, when media magnate Kerry Packer signed up most of Australia's Test cricketers, along with other outstanding world players, and paid them to compete in tournaments wearing brightly colored uniforms (green and gold for Australia) in place of the traditional all-white gear. The customary red ball was replaced by a white one for easier viewing under floodlights — themselves a radical departure from convention. The Packer circus endured for only two years, but some of the innovations it sponsored have now entered the mainstream of Australian cricket.

Soccer in all its Australian variety remains the most popular spectator sport. Four different versions are played: soccer, two versions of Rugby — Rubgy Union, the running-and-passing game played with 15 on a side, and Rugby League, the pared-down professional game with 13 men on each team — and Australian Rules, an indigenous version of soccer that is

played by teams 18-strong on an oversize field. Aussie Rules, which focuses on spectacular high kicking, marking and hand-passing, dominates the southern states and has by far the largest and most fanatical following of the four games. In Victoria, the performance of the clubs belonging to the 11-team league is a matter of passionate concern for the 150,000 highly partisan spectators who attend matches each Saturday, and once a year, the city of Melbourne virtually shuts down for the VFL (Victorian Football League) Grand Final, which draws crowds of more than 100,000 people.

As Australian society has changed, so have its sports heroes. Once it used to produce world champions from social groups that were fighting their way up the social ladder: Two of Australia's most famous folk heroes are Les Darcy and Dave Sands, middleweight boxers

who were from Irish and Aboriginal backgrounds respectively. But its heroes now tend to come from middle-class families and to excel in cool, technical skills, such as auto racing, in which the nation has produced world champions Jack Brabham and Alan Jones, and surfing, which is now in competition with the traditional surf lifesaving movement as Australia's national sport.

The switch is symbolic. The lifesaving clubs — voluntary organizations dedicated to helping swimmers in distress — tend to be authoritarian and heavily masculine, based on one particular beach. In their rituals of mateyness and team discipline, they reflect the movement's working-class origins. But since the beginning of the 1970s, they have lost many members to the more freewheeling and individualistic cult of surfing, aimed at self-fulfillment rather than community service.

At one time, any male teenager growing up in a beachside suburb would have gravitated naturally toward the local surf club. These days, however, youngsters living near the beaches, male and female, are more likely to purchase surfboards and then spend their time driving up and down the coast in borrowed cars in search of good waves. No better example could be found of the transitions that have occurred in Australia — from group activities to individual pursuits, from discipline to freedom, from working class to middle class, from the authentically Australian to the stylishly imported. And it is the new trend, with its sense of glamor and social mobility, that most attracts the attention of the media.

The media in Australia are, for the most part, commercially run, and ownership of the principal outlets is heavily concentrated. Four powerful chains dominate the nation's television, press and radio. Just three of them — John Fairfax Limited, Rupert Murdoch's News Corporation, and the Herald & Weekly Times Limited — own every daily newspaper in the state capital cities. Together with the fourth chain, Consolidated Press, they control eight of the nation's 15 city commercial TV stations, most of the suburban press, nearly all the national magazines and a large slice of Australian radio, putting them among the biggest corporations in all of Australia. With the introduction of Australia's domestic satellite in 1985 and the development of cable and subscription television, they can channel their programs into even the remotest outback home and are likely to extend their influence still further.

In theory, the power of the private media chains is balanced by the Aus-

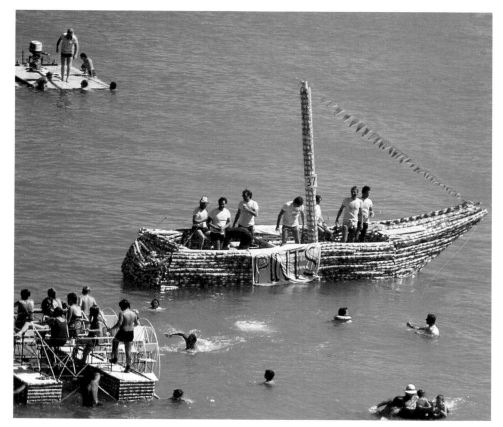

tralian Broadcasting Commission, a government-financed statutory authority that operates 10 television stations and 123 radio stations. The ABC is obliged by charter to take an even-handed approach to politics and social issues, but all its programs are upscale, aimed at minority-interest audiences, and generally command much smaller figures than the commercial networks. The ABC is also greatly outnumbered. In Adelaide, for example, there are three ABC radio stations and one ABC television channel in competition with five commercial radio stations and three commercial TV channels.

The concentration of media owner-

ship has inevitably led to criticism, particularly among Labor Party supporters, who raise charges of political bias; only twice in this century has any major daily newspaper endorsed Labor for a federal election. Another common complaint, directed particularly at the television stations, is that many programs aim at the lowest common denominator in public taste — hence the common perception that the best viewing to be found on Australian TV is the advertisements, which are often irreverent, sexy and imaginative. Although in 1981 the average household turned on its television set for approximately 32 hours a week, the Australian Broadcasting Tribunal has consistently found high levels of discontent among viewers. A Melbourne survey in 1975 found that 59 percent of respondents were dissatisfied with television programming and only 36 percent were satisfied; an advertising survey in 1977 found that the main problems of concern to Australians were: first, high prices; second, strikes; and third, the poor quality of television programs.

As a result, there are those who claim that the products of the Australian media are less interesting than the people who run them. The most celebrated of these is Rupert Murdoch, Australia's best-known media magnate. A part-heir to the newspaper chain built up by his father, Murdoch began his career with the Adelaide *News.* In 1964, displaying the business acumen that has characterized his career ever since, he used the secure financial base provided by the *News* to set up *The Australian,* the first genuinely national daily paper. To solve the problem of distribution in such a large country, Murdoch based the paper in Canberra and flew the printing plates out to the distant state capitals each night; later, new technology was used to print the paper simultaneously in several cities.

A strike called by newspaper journalists in 1975 to protest management's interference in editorial matters badly damaged *The Australian's* circulation,

At a neighborhood gathering in Perth, guests cluster around the barbecue to check on the progress of their sausages and steaks. A hospitable climate and comfortable living standard combine to make alfresco parties an enjoyable part of the Australian summer.

which fell from 153,000 in 1974 to 110,000 four years later. But by that time, Murdoch had moved into the television, mining and airline businesses and had developed international media interests as well.

In 1969, Murdoch bought the ailing *Sun* in England. By deliberately "going under" his rivals in terms of sex and sensationalism, with a topless pin-up girl on page 3 of the paper every day, he managed to boost circulation from 950,000 to four million. He had already acquired the *News of the World,* Britain's largest-selling Sunday newspaper, and later added the venerable *Times of London* and the *Sunday Times,* both at the other end of the market.

Murdoch also turned his sights on the United States. In New York, an eclectic series of acquisitions included the radical *Village Voice,* the mouthpiece of bohemian Greenwich Village, and the mass-circulation *New York Post.* In the latter case, however, the results of his stewardship were ambiguous. With a policy of brash and sensational news coverage, he lifted the *Post's* circulation, but he could not attract advertisers. According to one local paper, a buyer for one of New York's most prestigious stores told him: "Rupert, Rupert, your readers are our shoplifters."

Murdoch is not the only Australian media tycoon to have achieved international celebrity. Kerry Packer is another. Like Murdoch, Packer had inherited a media group from his father. The legacy included TV Channel 9 in Melbourne and Sydney, which he has expanded and consolidated, largely from the enormous profits generated after the introduction of color television to Australia in 1975. One of Packer's publishing ventures is a women's magazine called *Cleo,* containing sealed

sections, which, when opened along the dotted line, reveal sexually explicit articles and illustrations.

Apart from these ventures and the cricket circus — which he started when the Australian Cricket Board refused to give his television network exclusive rights to coverage of a Test series — Packer has invested heavily in mineral exploration, property development and gambling ventures such as Lotto.

The export of honest-to-goodness vulgarity by Australia's press magnates has done little for Australia's cultural reputation internationally, yet the fact is that there has not been such a flowering of the arts in Australia since the turn of the century. The 1890s saw a tremendous upsurge of nationalism, which was reflected in the development of identifiable national movements in literature, painting and drama. The growth of an authentic Australian voice was particularly apparent in its literature: This was the age of the bush balladers whose work was published in the *Bulletin* magazine — including Banjo Paterson, who wrote the ballad *The Man from Snowy River,* a well-loved anthology piece that was used as the basis for a feature film in 1982. It was also the time of Henry Lawson, probably Australia's finest short-story writer, and of novelists such as Joseph Furphy, the author of the picaresque *Such is Life.*

In the early 20th century, however, Australia's artistic voice faltered. By the 1950s, Australian culture had become essentially a derivative of larger English-speaking democracies: Most of its books, films, television programs and popular music were secondhand, imported from Britain or the United States. There was no lack of native energy and talent in Australia itself, but

A 50-foot-high Christmas tree stands behind a charity-collections box in Sydney's Martin Place. Although Christmas arrives Down Under at the height of summer, Australians still celebrate it in Northern European style, even sending cards showing robins chirping in the snow.

the general public was suspicious of original creation blossoming in their midst, tending to denigrate or patronize any homemade artistic endeavors. Another problem to be taken into account was that the audience for cultural activities was not a large one. The total population of Australia at the time was only about 7.5 million — less than that of New York City.

The lack of an audience and the depressing philistinism of much of Australian life during this period made many artists leave the country in order to pursue their careers in the great metropolitan centers overseas. Among the expatriates were painters Sydney Nolan, William Dobell, Arthur Boyd and Russell Drysdale, who were creating what was later to be labeled the "Australian School." In the field of perform-

5

ing arts, Robert Helpmann was in London developing his career as a dancer and, later, as a choreographer, and Joan Sutherland was building a reputation as one of the world's great opera singers. Malcolm Williamson, the composer, and Ray Lawler, the playwright, also went off to England so that they could make names for themselves.

But many creative talents, especially the writers, chose to stay on and fight for recognition in their homeland. By the 1960s, A. D. Hope—an academic poet in the classical tradition—R. D. Fitzgerald and Judith Wright were publishing contemporary poetry, and their work was being included in school syllabuses. Hal Porter had established his reputation as a formidable short-story writer and a virtuoso of language. Australia's foremost literary talent, Patrick White, had returned from London soon after World War II and was writing his early novels and plays; many of them, such as *The Tree of Man* and *Voss*, were set in a bush landscape. Younger novelists — such as Randolph Stow, Thea Astley, Peter Mathers and Thomas Keneally — were beginning to have their work published. The first significant Australian plays and movies were being produced.

It was an exciting and challenging time for artists, a period of adventure and breakthrough, but the audience, generally, remained small and comparatively unsophisticated. Painters, film makers, writers — all were members of a minority battling desperately against what Australian commentator Ronald Conway called, in the title of a book he wrote on the nation, *The Great Australian Stupor*. The drone of the yahoo and the philistine was still to be heard throughout the land.

But things were changing for the

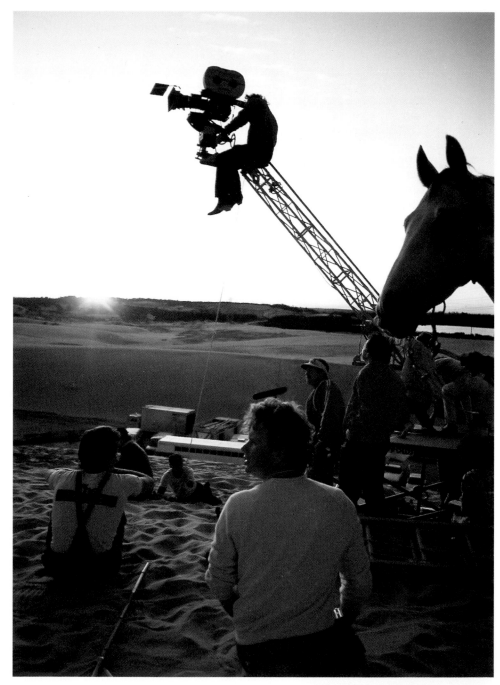

On location outside Sydney, a camera crew prepares to shoot a scene for a film about Phar Lap, a legendary race-horse of the 1930s. The renaissance of the movie industry dates from 1969, when the Australian Film Commission was formed; in the next decade more than 200 feature films were made.

144

Australians. The 1960s and 1970s were a period of economic expansion, high employment, increasing leisure time and growing national self-confidence. The historian H. D. Nicolson described it as an age of democratic imperialism, in which "dominating scale, luxurious finish and costly embellishment were necessary for the friendly flattery of the two rulers, people and leaders." The Sydney Opera House, most of the new arts complexes in the capital cities, and much of the city of Canberra itself were built during these two decades. Economic prosperity in a country is often associated with an increase in cultural energy, mainly because people have more time and money to spend on the arts, and Australia was no exception to the general rule.

At the same time, the nation's isolation from the outside world was suddenly broken by an immigration program that attracted millions of Britons and other Europeans to its shores. Cheaper air fares and technological developments in the media — color television sets, the cassette player, satellite communications — helped the process. State-administered censorship virtually disappeared, allowing artists to create work as lively and irreverent as that produced in London or New York. A continent hanging off the southern half of the globe, which expatriate writer Murray Sayle had described as being "As Far As You Can Go," suddenly found it had become part of the global village.

The effect of all these changes was to transform Australia from a cultural backwater into a major participant in the international world of the arts. Few people, for example, could have foreseen in the 1960s that in little more than a decade, the Australian movie industry would become one of the most visible of all national film industries. Aided partly by money from the government and by patronage, including the introduction of tax-benefit plans for film investors and the setting up of the Australian Film Development Corporation, the industry has created works as various as *Picnic at Hanging Rock, Gallipoli, Breaker Morant, Newsfront, The Man from Snowy River, My Brilliant Career* and the *Mad Max* series. In 1976, Bruce Petty, the cartoonist, won an Oscar for the best animated film, a short humorous work entitled *Leisure*. In literature, Patrick White won the Nobel Prize in 1973, and Thomas Keneally won the 1982 Booker Prize, Britain's most prestigious literary award, for his *Schindler's Ark*, recounting the story of a German businessman who had secretly helped Jews in Nazi Germany. The poetry of Les Murray, who has written long and moving celebrations of the central-coast district of New South Wales, of Peter Porter, an expatriate poet living in London, and of A. D. Hope is studied at universities throughout Europe and the United States.

At a more popular level of the arts, Jim Sharman, the stage and movie director, took *Jesus Christ Superstar* and *The Rocky Horror Picture Show* and turned them into mammoth entertainment successes all over the world. Australian rock groups have entered the record charts in the United States and in England. Satirist Barry Humphries has had such a success with send-ups of archetypical Aussie characters — most notably Dame Edna Everage, "housewife superstar" — that he divides his time between London and Portugal, paying only fleeting visits to the country that is the source of his inspiration. Include the successes of the long-established greats — the Sutherlands, Helpmanns and Williamsons — and it seems that, for such a small population, Australia's achievement in the arts almost rivals its achievement in sports.

However, to judge the arts by their fame overseas is to indulge in what Australians disparagingly refer to as the "cultural cringe" — the assumption that artistic works have merit only if they have achieved success abroad. Most of the action occurs at home, and foreign audiences rarely get to hear about it. The theater, for instance, has been through an extraordinary renaissance, but many of the plays written by local dramatists are so unabashedly Australian in their theme and language that only a handful have been performed elsewhere. Ray Lawler's *Summer of the Seventeenth Doll*, about Queensland cane cutters, and Alan Seymour's *The One Day of the Year*, an exploration of the generation gap as exposed by Anzac Day, were the forerunners of this movement. It did not achieve its full expression, however, until the early 1970s, when radical political drama appeared for the first time in Melbourne at two experimental theaters, La Mama's and the Pram Factory.

The playwrights who emerged then went on to become the nation's leading dramatists: Jack Hibberd, whose one-man play *A Stretch of the Imagination*, a virtuoso piece that takes a laconic look at the nation's bush and mateship traditions, is one of the finest pieces of theater written in Australia; and David Williamson, who has written a series of satirical plays, including *The Club*, about wheeling and dealing in Australian Rules soccer, and *Don's Party*, a play — and later a film — about "upwardly mobile" Labor supporters attending a raucous election-eve party.

5

Australian painting and sculpture have had more international success than the theater, but again the most important creative work has been done inside the country. Until his death in 1982, Fred Williams was a dominant figure, and arguably the best landscape painter in a tradition that includes such major figures as Tom Roberts, Arthur Streeton and Russell Drysdale. In the course of a lifetime's prolific work, Williams created an abstract yet recognizable vision of the bush that has become as pervasive in the iconography of the country as the earlier sunlight-and-gum-trees imagery of Hans Heysen. Williams' vision is darker and less sentimental, but equally celebratory.

In literature, three trends have become apparent. One is the appearance of a new generation of talented women, of whom Helen Garner is typical. Her novel *Monkey Grip,* later turned into a successful movie, takes a close-up look at contemporary inner-city life — drugs, feminism, rock music, the attempt to pursue an alternative lifestyle in a Melbourne ghetto. The second has been a definitive move away from the highly wrought style and symbolism that is characteristic of Patrick White, who nevertheless remains the dominant figure in Australian literature. A third significant development has been the resurgence of the short story as a major form of literature, with writers such as Peter Carey, Murray Bail, Frank Moorhouse, Peter Cowan, Beverley Farmer and James McQueen revitalizing a tradition begun by Henry Lawson and the *Bulletin* school in the 1890s. Their best work tends to be laconic, experimental and urban, characterized by irony.

Classical music, opera and ballet all expanded during the 1970s, although in the 1980s there was a cutback in federal-government subsidies to the performing arts. Music has always tended to be more energetic in performance than in composition, and Australia has produced several major orchestras, chamber groups and opera companies. Composers such as Richard Meale, Peter Sculthorpe, Anne Boyd, Moya Henderson, Nigel Butterley and Graham Koehne, however, have their new work performed by local groups, and they are helped by occasional commissions from the Australian Broadcasting Commission, which is the main outlet for orchestral music.

The arts in Australia today are viable, visible and popular, and the cultural ferment they reflect may indeed suggest that the nation still deserves its famous sobriquet of "the lucky country." Today's Australians have inherited a continent that has the climate, the natural resources and the sort of living standards that European navigators and explorers could never have dreamed of when they set out in small, leaky sailing ships to discover the Great South Land. Not that the country is a South Pacific utopia of the sort that Tahiti once promised to be; it is too vast, too extreme and too challenging for that. One of the nation's most popular ski resorts is a valley that early bushmen named The Perisher for its threatening and intractable climate. Its present comfortable affluence is both a result and a symbol of the brute determination of the earlier generations of European settlers to make the most of what this alien, un-European and sometimes hostile continent had to offer.

Australia began its modern history as one of the worst penal colonies in the world. In less than two centuries it has developed into a wealthy, suburban society characterized by some commentators as perhaps the most middle-class of all nations. Yet other voices have been raised to point out shortcomings. Since the early 1970s, Australia, like many Western countries, has been hit by high unemployment, inflation, recession and damaging political crises. Some say that the old Australian traditions of egalitarianism and opportunity for all have been submerged beneath a more ruthless and competitive ethic, and that the extremes of society have drawn further apart. Certainly Australia has become more and more like other developed societies: It must confront pollution, social divisiveness, violence, exploitation, welfare lines and the universal threat of nuclear war.

And yet the nation feels optimistic. In their everyday lives, most Australians still display a lively affirmation of life. There are lines of people eager to spend money in the supermarkets and sun-oiled bodies strewn on the beaches. On weekends, families load up the car and head for the coast, or the outback, or a visit to the "oldies," as parents are affectionately known. At the end of each year, the schools graduate hundreds of thousands of turbulent, unfazed, cosmopolitan youngsters, some now with Mediterranean features or Asian skins, who disappear into jobs or colleges, or overseas — although some will end up on welfare.

At heart, they are a cheerful and pleasure-loving people, and as 19th-century British historian J. A. Froude described it after visiting the country, "It is hard to quarrel with men who only wish to be innocently happy." One can only wonder whether the end of the explosive 20th century will allow that happiness to continue undisturbed. □

URBAN STREET ART

Girls playing basketball in a Sydney playground blend with a background mural.

A bush scene brightens up a garage.

A Darwin youth pauses by an Art Deco face.

In Alice Springs, women pass a supermarket mural depicting vignettes of outback life.

The desire to beautify Australia's urban sprawl has produced a crop of striking murals in towns across the nation. The boldly colored works are usually commissioned by municipal authorities, and the artists draw inspiration from sources as diverse as fashion magazines and surrealist art. Particularly popular are scenes of life in the outback, featuring such picturesque motifs as windmills and the camels that used to serve as draft animals in desert areas.

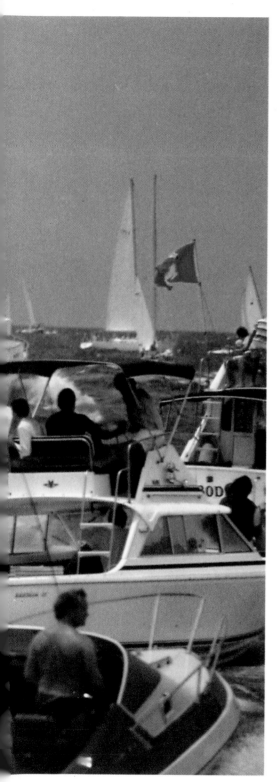

THE OCEAN PLAYGROUND

A warm climate and a welcoming coastline have made the sea Australia's playground. Each summer, hundreds of thousands of sun-loving hedonists head daily for the sand, which is usually within easy reach; three quarters of the population lives within 50 miles of the shore, and Sydney alone has 30 ocean beaches.

Aside from the universal pleasures of swimming and sunbathing, boating ranks as the most popular marine recreation. As far back as early colonial times, rowing contests were held between rival crews in ships' longboats. Leisure sailing developed in the course of the 19th century, and now squadrons of amateur sailors weigh anchor every weekend in a plethora of craft ranging from 13-foot-long skiffs to motorboats and even to ocean-going yachts. Racing remains popular, and the international competitiveness of the nation's yachtsmen was confirmed in 1983, when *Australia II* defeated the yacht *Liberty* and became the first vessel in 132 years to wrest the America's Cup from the United States.

Surfing, an art originating among Pacific islanders and popularized in the United States, developed into a nationwide craze in Australia after the introduction of lightweight boards in the 1950s. Soon it had its own jargon and lifestyle, as well as heroes such as Bernard "Midget" Farrelly of New South Wales, who became surfing's first world champion in 1964. Today about 500,000 Australians surf, but the sport's predominance is challenged by the growing vogue for windsurfing, a variation of conventional sailing that adds some of the thrills of boat handling to the surfer's close communion with the waves.

Crew members of an American yacht participating in the 660-mile Sydney to Hobart Race sit with their legs dangling over the side of their heeling vessel while spectator craft escort them out of Sydney Harbor. The race attracts some 80 yachts annually in spite of high seas and gale-force winds.

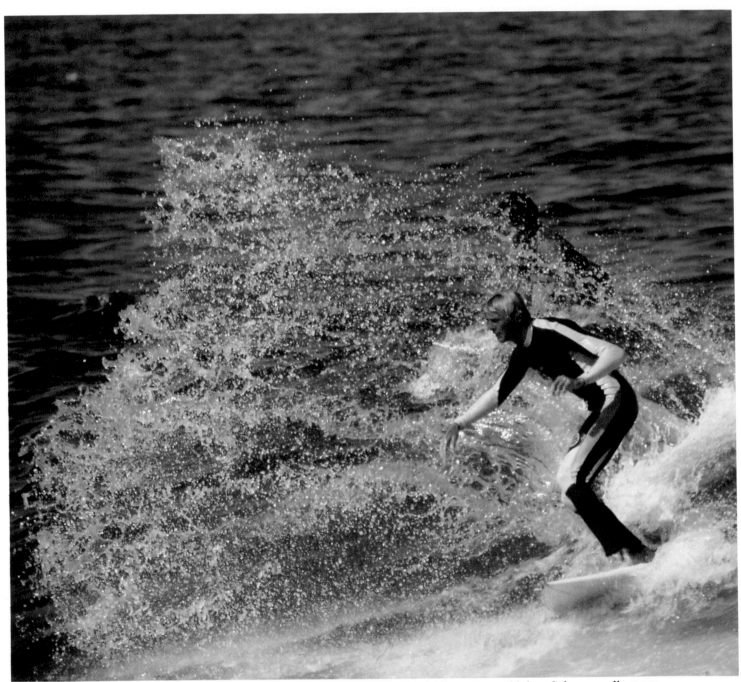

Shooting the waves at Manly Beach, a northern suburb of Sydney, a wetsuited surfer deftly maneuvers his board along a curling wave.

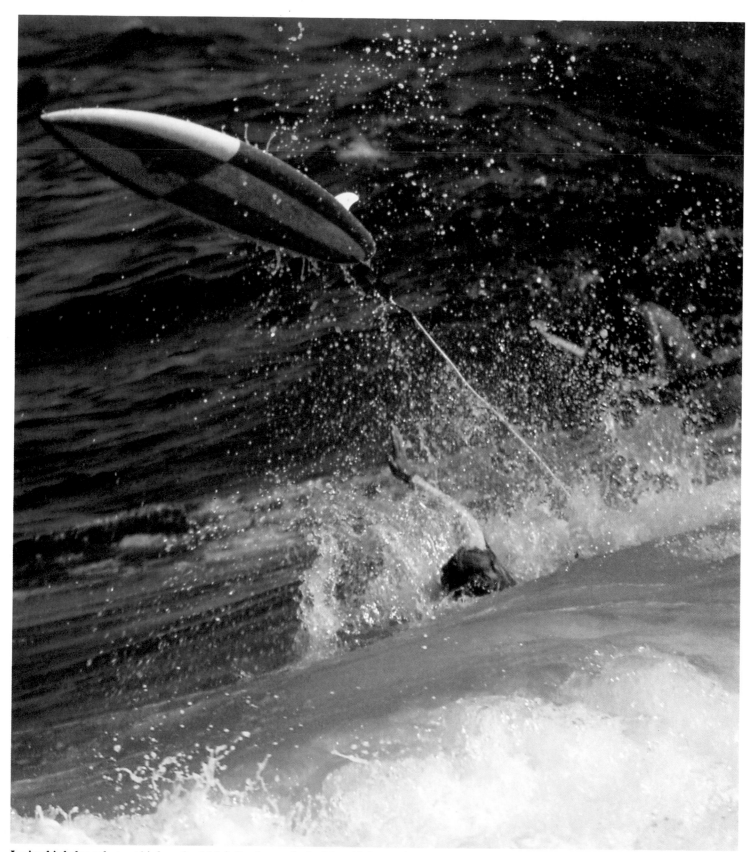

Losing his balance but not his board, which is firmly attached to his ankle by a tether, the same surfer wipes out a few moments later.

At the start of the windsurfing race that is part of the annual Festival of Sydney, an armada of entrants sets off from Manly Beach. Popular since the late 1960s, windsurfing has rapidly become a competitive sport: Fleets entering national- and world-title contests may have as many as 200 participants.

The wooded cliffs of Barranjoey Head at the north end of Palm Beach in New South Wales loom behind a windsurfer as he controls his slight craft in a stiff breeze. To steer the 10-foot-long, 60-pound polyurethane board, the surfer changes the sail's position with the help of a wishbone-shaped boom.

A flotilla of pleasure boats led by a majestic schooner surrounds six ferryboats competing in the Sydney Harbor Ferrython, a lighthearted event in the January-long Sydney Festival. Ferry service linking outlying districts with the city center began in the 19th century, and despite competition from cars and hydrofoils, it still provides commuters from some suburbs with an attractively old-fashioned way of crossing the congested metropolis.

ACKNOWLEDGMENTS

The index for this book was prepared by Vicki Robinson. For their help in the preparation of this volume, the editors wish to thank: Agent General for South Australia, London; Agent General for Victoria, London; Library, Australian High Commission, London; Australian Tourist Commission, London; Francesca Baas-Becking, Australian Institute of Aboriginal Studies, Canberra; Baiba Berzins, Mitchell Library, State Library of New South Wales, Sydney; Broken Hill Proprietary Co. Ltd., London; John W. Brown, Government of Western Australia, London; Chartair, Alice Springs; Flinders Bookshop, London; Freshwater Surf Life Saving Club, Sydney; Noel Fullerton, Virginia Camel Safaris, Alice Springs; Alistair J. Gilmour, Great Barrier Reef Marine Park Authority, Townsville, Queensland; Anne-Louise Graham Bell, Sydney; Fred Hockley, Director, School of the Air, Alice Springs; Elizabeth Hodgson, London; Keith Hope, Department of State Development, South Australian Government, Adelaide; H. L. Keelan, Broken Hill Library, City of Broken Hill, New South Wales; Stephen Langhorn, Agent General for New South Wales, London; Jimmy Lucas, Department of Photographs, Imperial War Museum, London; Heinz Luik, Alice Springs Federal Casino, Alice Springs; Brian Males, Royal Flying Doctor Service, Alice Springs; Librarian, Botany Department, Natural History Museum, London; North Crenella Surf Life Saving Club, Sydney; North Narabeen Surf Life Saving Club, Sydney; Reg O'Grady, Agent General for Queensland, London; Mike O'Hanlan, Museum of Mankind, London; Queenscliffe Surf Life Saving Club, Sydney; K. A. Richards, North Broken Hill Holdings Ltd., Melbourne; Malcolm Roberts, Cattlemen's Association, Alice Springs; Frank Strahan, The University of Melbourne Archives, Carlton, Victoria; Bill and June Tapp, Killarney Station, Northern Territory; Public Relations Director, University of Sydney; Bob Watt, *The Centralian*, Alice Springs.

PICTURE CREDITS

Credits from left to right are separated by semicolons, from top to bottom by dashes.

Cover: Boulton-Wilson from the Daily Telegraph Colour Library, London. Front endpaper: Map by Roger Stewart, London. Back endpaper: Digitized image by Creative Data, London.

1, 2: © Flag Research Center, Winchester, Massachusetts. 6, 7: Patrick Ward, London. 8-11: Hans Wiesenhofer, Pöllau, Austria, insets, Digitized image by Creative Data, London. 12, 13: Roger Garwood, Fremantle, Western Australia. 14, 15: Jean-Paul Ferrero, Canberra, inset, Digitized image by Creative Data, London. 16: Patrick Ward, London. 18: Paul Simcock from The Image Bank, New York; John Garrett, London; Richard Woldendorp from Photo Index, Perth, Western Australia. 19: Patrick Ward, London; J. M. La-Roque from The Image Bank, New York; Roger Garwood, Fremantle. 20: Jean-Paul Ferrero, Canberra; Jen and Des Bartlett from Bruce Coleman Ltd., Uxbridge, Middlesex — Jean-Paul Ferrero, Canberra. 21: Jean-Paul Ferrero, Canberra. 22: Digitized image by Creative Data, London. 23: John Garrett, London — Alan Jones from The Image Bank, New York. 25: Patrick Ward, London. 26: John Garrett, London; Hans Wiesenhofer, Pöllau, Austria. 27: John Garrett, London; Gunther Deichmann, Melbourne. 29: Detail of *The Selector's Hut (Whelan on the Log)* by Arthur Streeton, 1890. Collection: Australian National Gallery, Canberra. 31: Cary Wolinsky from Stock, Boston. 33: Georg Gerster from The John Hillelson Agency, London; John Banagan from The Image Bank, New York. 34: John Garrett, London. 35: Guy Lamothe, Melbourne. 36, 37: Jean-Paul Ferrero, Canberra. 38: Jo Daniell, Melbourne. 39: Edward Stokes, Queanbeyan, New South Wales. 40: David Goulston from Bruce Coleman Ltd., Uxbridge, Middlesex. 41, 42: Jean-Paul Ferrero, Canberra. 43: David Moore, Sydney. 44: Jean-Paul Ferrero, Canberra. 45: Penny Tweedie from Colorific!, London. 46, 47: Australia House, courtesy of E. T. Archive, London. 48: Portrait of Captian Cook by Sir Nathaniel Dance, courtesy of the National Maritime Museum's Greenwich Hospital Collection, London. 49: Sketch by Sydney Parkinson from The British Library, London (Add. MS 9345 f. 16v). 50, 51: The British Museum (Natural History), London. 52: BBC Hulton Picture Library, London — From the log book of the *Lady Penrhyn* from The British Library, London (Add. MS 47966 ff. 5v-6). 53: Cartoon from Melbourne *Punch* from E. T. Archive, London. 54: Portrait of Arthur Phillip by F. Wheatley, 1786, courtesy of the National Portrait Gallery, London; from *South Australia Illustrated* by George French Angas, Royal Commonwealth Society Library, London, courtesy of E. T. Archive, London — BBC Hulton Picture Library, London. 55: Australian Stamp Bureau, London, on behalf of Australia Post; Philip Quirk from The Image Bank, New York — Patrick Ward, London. 56-57: Digitized image by Creative Data, London; *Overland Expedition Leaving Adelaide 1844*, by Samuel Thomas Gill, courtesy of the Art Gallery of South Australia, Adelaide. 59: *Battle of Eureka*, by B. Ireland, courtesy of E. T. Archive, London. 61: Mary Evans Picture Library, London; BBC Hulton Picture Library, London. 62: BBC Hulton Picture Library, London. 65: Imperial War Museum, London *(top and center)* — Australian War Memorial, Canberra. 66: John Garrett, London. 67: D. and J. Heaton from Colorific!, London — Digitized image by Creative Data, London. 68-73: *Impressions of Broken Hill 1908-1910*, courtesy of Edward Stokes, Queanbeyan, New South Wales. 74, 75: Cary Wolinsky from Stock, Boston. 76: Roger Garwood, Fremantle. 77: Gunther Deichmann, Melbourne. 78, 79: Roger Garwood, Fremantle. 80: Gunther Deichmann, Melbourne. 81: Cary Wolinsky from Stock, Boston. 82, 83: Patrick Ward, London. 84: Alastair Scott, Fochabers, Scotland. 85: Pierre Boulat from Cosmos, Paris. 86: Gunther Deichmann, Melbourne. 87: Alastair Scott, Fochabers, Scotland. 88: Gunther Deichmann, Melbourne — Roger Garwood, Fremantle. 89: Roger Garwood, Fremantle — Gunther Deichmann, Melbourne. 90, 91: Cary Wolinsky from Stock, Boston. 92: John Garrett, London. 94: Nick Bade © LIFE 1984/Time Inc. from Colorific!, London. 95: Edward Stokes, Queanbeyan, New South Wales. 96: David Austen from Bruce Coleman Ltd., Uxbridge, Middlesex. 97: Jean-Paul Ferrero, Canberra. 98: Penny Tweedie, London. 99: Penny Tweedie from Focus Talentbank, Hamburg. 100, 101: Richard Woldendorp from Photo Index, Perth. 102, 103: John Garrett, London. 104: Patrick Ward, London. 105: Penny Tweedie, London. 106, 107: John Peel, Sydney. 108, 109: Patrick Ward, London. 110: Alastair Scott, Fochabers, Scotland. 113: Jean-Paul Ferrero, Canberra. 114-116: Patrick Ward, London. 117: Paul Wright from Photo Index, Perth. 118: Roger Garwood, Fremantle. 119: Patrick Ward, London. 120, 121: Roger Garwood, Fremantle. 122-126: Penny Tweedie from Colorific!, London. 127-129: Jean-Paul Ferrero, Canberra. 130, 131: Pierre Boulat from Cosmos, Paris. 132, 133: John Garrett, London. 134: Jean-Paul Ferrero, Canberra — J. M. La-Roque from The Image Bank, New York. 135: Michael Coyne from The Image Bank, New York. 136: Jean-Paul Ferrero, Canberra. 137-139: Patrick Ward, London. 140: John Garrett, London. 141: Gunther Deichmann, Melbourne. 142: Cary Wolinsky from Stock, Boston. 143: Patrick Ward, London. 144: David Parker from The Image Bank, New York. 147-151: Patrick Ward, London, except 147 bottom left, Alastair Scott, Fochabers, Scotland. 152: David Moore, Sydney. 153: John Garrett, London. 154, 155: Jean-Paul Ferrero, Canberra.

BIBLIOGRAPHY

BOOKS
Aitken, Jonathan, *Land of Fortune*. London: Martin Secker & Warburg, 1971.
Allen, Oliver E., and the Editors of Time-Life Books, *The Pacific Navigators* (The Seafarers series). Alexandria, Va.: Time-Life Books, 1980.
Australian Mineral Industry Annual Review for 1981. Australian Government Publishing Service, 1984.
Baglin, Douglass, and Barbara Mullins, *The Book of Australia*. Sydney: Summit Books, 1973.
Berndt, Ronald M., ed., *Australian Aboriginal Art*. Middlesex, England: Collier-Macmillan, 1964.
Blainey, Geoffrey:
The Rise of Broken Hill. London: Macmillan, 1968.
Triumph of the Nomads. London: The Macmillan Press, 1976.
Boehm, A. E., *Twentieth Century Economic Development in Australia*. Melbourne: Longman Cheshire, 1971.
Broom, Leonard, and F. Lancaster Jones, *A Blanket a Year*. Australian National University Press, 1973.
Burton, Barbara, and William Splatt, *100 Masterpieces of Australian Painting*. Australia: John Currey O'Neil Publishers, 1981.
Cameron, R. J., *Year Book Australia*. Australian Bureau of Statistics, 1983.
Carroll, John B., ed., *Intruders in the Bush*. Oxford University Press, 1982.
Chisholm, A. H., and Vincent Serventy, *John Gould's the Birds of Australia*. Sydney: Lansdowne Press,

1973.

Cobbe, Hugh, ed., *Cook's Voyages and Peoples of the Pacific*. British Museum Publications, 1979.

Coghill, I., *Australia's Mineral Resources*. Sorrett Publishers, 1971.

Cornelia, Elizabeth, *Australia: The Land and Its People*. London: Macdonald Educational, 1977.

Crowley, Frank, ed., *A New History of Australia*. Melbourne: Heinemann, 1974.

Davies, David M., *The Last of the Tasmanians*. London: Frederick Muller, 1973.

Flood, Josephine, *Archaeology of the Dreamtime*. Sydney: William Collins, 1983.

Fodor's Australia, New Zealand and the South Pacific. London: Hodder & Stoughton, 1984.

Fraser, Bryce, *The Macquarie Book of Australian Events*. The Macquarie Library, 1983.

Griffin, J., ed., *Essays in the Economic History of Australia*. Jacaranda Press, 1967.

A History of Commerce and Industry in Western Australia. University of Western Australia Press, 1981.

Horne, Donald, *The Lucky Country*. London: Penguin Books, 1964.

Howard, Colin, *Australia's Constitution*. Australia: Penguin Books, 1978.

Hughes, Robert, *The Art of Australia*. London: Penguin Books, 1970.

Idriess, Ion L., *Lasseter's Last Ride*. London: Jonathan Cape, 1936.

Kearns, R.H.B., *Broken Hill: A Pictorial History*. Australia: Investigator Press, 1982.

Keneally, Thomas, *Outback*. London: Hodder & Stoughton, 1983.

Kynaston, Edward, *The Penguin Book of the Bush*. London: Penguin Books, 1977.

Lacour-Gayet, Robert, *A Concise History of Australia*. London: Penguin Books, 1976.

Laffin, John, *Anzacs at War*. London: Abelard-Schuman, 1965.

McGregor, Craig:
The Australian People. New South Wales: Hodder & Stoughton, 1980.
Profile of Australia. London: Penguin Books, 1968.

McGregor, Craig, and the Editors of Time-Life Books, *The Great Barrier Reef* (The World's Wild Places series). Amsterdam: Time-Life Books, 1974.

McLeod, A. L., ed., *The Pattern of Australian Culture*. New York: Cornell University Press, 1963.

McLuckie, John, and H. S. McKee, *Australian and New Zealand Botany*. Sydney: Horwitz Publications Inc., 1954.

Marshall, Catherine, *Thorn Bird Country*. London: Thames & Hudson, 1983.

Minerals and Mineral Development. Department of Resources Development, Western Australia, 1984.

Moffitt, Ian, and the Editors of Time-Life Books, *The Australian Outback* (The World's Wild Places series). Amsterdam: Time-Life Books, 1976.

Morcombe, Michael, *An Illustrated Encyclopaedia of Australian Wildlife*. Melbourne: The Macmillan Company of Australia, 1974.

Nomination of the Great Barrier Reef for Inclusion in the World Heritage List. Great Barrier Reef Marine Park Authority, 1981.

Norton, W. R., *The Deterioration in Economic Performance*. Reserve Bank of Australia.

OECD Economic Surveys 1982-1983, Australia. OECD, 1983.

Paynting, H. H., ed., *The James Flood Book of Early Australian Photographs*. The James Flood Charity Trust, 1970.

Peach's Australian Cities. Australian Broadcasting Commission, 1980.

Pearling in Western Australia. Department of Fisheries & Wildlife, 1981.

Porter, Peter, and the Editors of Time-Life Books, *Sydney* (The Great Cities series). Amsterdam: Time-Life Books, 1980.

Queensland Resources Atlas. Brisbane: State Public Relations Bureau, 1980.

Rienits, Rex, and Thea Rienits:
A Pictorial History of Australia. Sydney: Paul Hamlyn, 1978.
The Voyages of Captain Cook. Middlesex, England: The Hamlyn Publishing Group, 1968.

Rodriguez de la Fuente, Felix, *Animals of Australasia*. London: Orbis, 1971.

Shaw, A.G.L., *The Story of Australia*. London: Faber & Faber, 1983.

Slater, Peter, *A Field Guide to Australian Birds*. Edinburgh: Scottish Academic Press, 1970.

Smith, Bernard, *Australian Painting 1788-1970*. Oxford University Press, 1971.

The South West Book: A Tasmanian Wilderness. Australian Conservation Commission, 1978.

Spearritt, Peter, and David Walker, eds., *Australian Popular Culture*. Australia: George Allen & Unwin, 1979.

Stokes, Edward, *United We Stand*. Australia: The Five Mile Press, 1983.

Stone, C. R., *Australian Landforms*. Australia: Wren Publishing, 1974.

Suter, Keith D., and Kaye Stearman, *Aboriginal Australians*. Minority Rights Group, 1982.

Sykes, T., *The Money Miners*. Wildcat Press, 1978.

Thiele, Colin, *The Adelaide Story*. Television Broadcasters Ltd., 1982.

This is Australia. Sydney: Lansdowne Press, 1982.

Thomas, Laurie, ed., *200 Years of Australian Painting*. Australia: Bay Books, 1971.

Tullock, John, *Australian Cinema*. Australia: George Allen & Unwin, 1982.

Ward, Russel, *The Australian Legend*. Oxford University Press, 1958.

Whitaker, Donald P., *Area Handbook for Australia*. The American University, 1974.

Wright, Judith, *The Cry for the Dead*. Oxford University Press, 1981.

Yeomans, John, *The Scarce Australians*. London: Longmans, Green & Co. Ltd., 1967.

PERIODICALS

Abercrombe, Thomas J., "Perth — Fair Winds and Full Sails." *National Geographic*, May 1982.

Brennan, Niall, "The Last of the Camel Men." *GEO* (Australia), June-August 1982.

The British Empire:
No. 11, "The World Revealed." Amsterdam: Time-Life Books, 1972.
No. 13, "Early Days Down Under," Amsterdam: Time-Life Books, 1972.
No. 42, "Australia Strikes It Rich." Amsterdam: Time-Life Books, 1972.
No. 43, "Opening the Outback." Amsterdam: Time-Life Books, 1972.

Burger, Angela, "Brisbane — A Little Bit Country." *GEO* (Australia), September-November 1982.

Canby, Thomas Y., "El Niño's Ill Wind." *National Geographic*, February 1984.

Caras, Roger, "What's a Koala?" *GEO* (U.S.A.), May 1983.

Duncan, Tim, "The Garden State Runs Dry." *The Bulletin*, January 18, 1983.

"Financial Times Survey — Australia," *Financial Times*, November 8, 1982.

Garwood, Roger, "Twenty Fathoms under the Sea." *Western Australia*, spring 1981.

Grenard, Philip, "Schools with a Dash of Color." *The Bulletin*, August 17, 1982.

Grenard, Philip, and Neil Speirs, "The New Asian Invasion." *The Bulletin*, August 16, 1983.

Guppy, Daryl, "White Cliffs, Dark Opals." *GEO* (Australia), March-May 1983.

Holmes, Rosemary, "White Man's Hole in the Ground." *GEO* (Australia), March-May 1983.

Hoyle, Russ, "Australia's 'Great Dry.'" *Time*, March 28, 1983.

"In the Deep End — Bob Hawke's Australia: A Survey." *The Economist*, August 6, 1983.

Knightley, Phillip:
"Once and Future Kings." *Sunday Times Magazine*, October 2, 1983.
"Skirmish in Paradise." *Sunday Times Magazine*, July 10, 1983.

McIlwraith, John, "Salt — The White Harvest." *Western Australia*, autumn 1982.

Moore, Kenny, "Coober Pedy — Opal Capital of Australia's Outback." *National Geographic*, October 1976.

Nicklin, Lenore, "The Wednesday Two States Burned to Ashes." *The Bulletin*, March 1, 1983.

"Save the Kangaroo." *The Listener*, March 8, 1984.

Schraps, Wolfgang, "Der Energie-Sparer." *GEO* (Germany), November 1982.

Scollay, Clive, "Arnhem Land Aboriginals Cling to Dreamtime." *National Geographic*, November 1980.

Segal, David, "Angels of the Outback." *GEO* (Australia), March-May 1982.

Souter, Gavin, "Bizarre Folk Hero." *Smithsonian*, June 1983.

Stevens, Joan, "Tasmania's South-West." *GEO* (Australia), 1980.

Stokes, Edward, "Broken Hill: Where Has All the Silver Gone?" *GEO* (Australia), 1979.

Templin, Jenny, "Lifesavers." *Journey*, December 1982-February 1983.

The Times: Times Special Report, September 15 and October 12, 1982.

Tropical Cyclone Warning Center, "Looking a Storm in the Eye." *GEO* (Australia), 1979.

White, Paul William, "At Grips with an Island State of Mind." *The Bulletin*, November 16, 1982.

Wilesmith, Greg, "Land Rights Become Reality." *The Bulletin*, May 10, 1983.

INDEX

Page numbers in italics refer to illustrations or to illustrated text.

Time-Life Books Inc. offers a wide range of fine recordings, including a *Rock 'n' Roll Era* series. For subscription information, call 1-800-445-TIME, or write TIME-LIFE MUSIC, Time & Life Building, Chicago, Illinois 60611.

JAVA

BALI

INDONESIA

TIMOR

ARAFURA SEA

MELVILLE ISLAND
BATHURST ISLAND

COVE
PENINSULA

Darwin

ARNHEM LAND

TIMOR SEA

JOSEPH
BONAPARTE
GULF

• Katherine

EY

INDIAN OCEAN

NORTHERN TERRITORY

• Broome

Tennant Creek●

NORTH WEST SHELF

● Port Hedland

● Marble Bar

• Dampier

● Alice Springs

Todd River

Tom Price●

● Newman

WESTERN AUSTRALIA

SHARK BAY

● Meekatharra

Oodnadatta●

Cöober Pedy●

SOUTH AUSTRALIA

Woomer

● Kalgoorlie

Coolgardie●

Perth   *Swan River*

● Fremantle

Why

GREAT AUSTRALIAN BIGHT

● Kwinana

Port Linc

EYRE
PENINSULA

Blackwood River

SPENCER GULF

KANGAROO ISLAND

SOUTHERN OCEAN